THE LORD'S FINANCIAL PLAN

THE LORD'S FINANCIAL PLAN

Gain
Financial Freedom!

JOSEPH E. SINGLETON
FINANCIAL PLANNER

BAC
P
Inc.

The Lord's Financial Plan – Gain Financial Freedom!
Joseph E. Singleton
Financial Planner

Cover design by Robbin Burrows
Book design by Larry Bledsoe

Published by: BAC Publishers, Inc.
                1749 W. 13th St.
                Upland, CA 91786

Printed in the United States of America

Disclaimer

This book is for educational purposes. It identifies the types of investments available but does not endorse any specific investment or warrant the performance thereof. Nor does it recommend any specific broker or dealer. It is not intended to take the place of advice from your financial planner, tax consultant, or legal advisor. Contact your financial planner to develop a plan that is right for you.

Library of Congress Control Number:
                  2007936191

ISBN: 978-0-9655730-8-5

First printing 2007

Bible Scriptures are from NKJV, The Living Bible, and NIV

Dedication

To my mom who encouraged me to be the best I can be and that there's nothing I cannot accomplish.

To my dad who taught me integrity, hard work, and commitment are the important "things" in life.

It was and is easy for me to accept Jesus' unconditional love from their examples.

Contents

Preface

1 John 1:4

And these things we write to you
that your joy may be full.

This book is intended to teach the basic fundamentals of financial planning from the Lord's perspective, and what our responsibility is to that perspective. It is written for those willing to learn what God expects from His followers in the area of finances and how to apply it in their daily lives.

The Lord talks a lot about money and possessions in the Bible. It would be an exhaustive volume of books to study every financial topic discussed in His Word. This particular book begins with the mindset that we should have about our finances. It will proceed into what financial planning is specifically and then finally into the individual categories of proper Biblical financial planning.

The difference in this book and a typical Bible study on money is that the everyday practical side of effective financial planning is explained in detail, but in a simple easy to understand way. The categories of financial planning are broken down into three main sections: protection, accumulation, and preservation. This book covers the products, the uses, the benefits of each, and the Bible teaching on each item. The intention is to be a resource for anyone who wants to know what true Biblical financial stewardship is.

Most of the items discussed cannot be accomplished without the assistance of a professional, i.e., a financial planner, accountant, or an estate planning attorney. After reading the material covered, you should be able to tell if they have your best interest at heart. You will learn that God expects us to understand how money works, and He expects us to actually execute the ideas mentioned.

The *intangible* aspects of money management are just as important as the *tangible* aspects. The intangibles are to have a mindset of being a steward and to realize everything is God's to begin with, to know how important it is to have a giving attitude, and lastly, to appreciate the value of leaving a legacy.

These concepts are not new because they came from the Bible; however, putting them together spiritually and practically is new. Doing what the Lord tells us to do will always result in His blessings. Read, learn, enjoy, implement, and fulfill God's destiny in your life!

Acknowledgments

I do not know how I can give proper credit to the people involved in the completion of this book. There cannot be a correct order or I fear offending someone. However, I must begin with Jesus Christ, my personal Lord and Savior, who gave me the idea of a simple easy-to-read book on the basics of financial planning for the church.

At the time it seemed like an impossibility that I was definitely not worthy of accomplishing. But the Holy Spirit gave me the wisdom, discernment, and perseverance to complete this daunting task.

I must thank Pastor Art Van Der Pol, who led me to the Lord and taught me the importance of discipleship. It was his idea originally for me to actually write a book after I discussed with him what I felt the Lord told me to do.

My church and my pastor, Pomona First Baptist and Glenn Gunderson, are incredible examples of what a church family should be like. They are supportive, caring, and generous. They speak the truth in love and ask everyone to change the world for Christ.

The Christian Community Credit Union welcomed me with open arms when I came aboard as a financial planner with them. This is a place where all the employees have a common goal and that is to serve the members with all their hearts. It really is a ministry and not just a place of employment.

My accountability partner, Jim Eriksen, has been such an amazing prayer warrior for me and my children. I would not have been able to finish this book without him.

My best friend, Mike Pedevill, has been there for me for almost eleven years now. We have both seen the highs and lows of what this life has to offer. Through the trials, we have seen God's amazing grace come pouring down on us and understand brokenness is truly a blessing from God.

I must thank Larry and Jane Bledsoe at BAC Publishers, Inc. for giving me the opportunity and their willingness to work with me. Also for all the corrections, encouragement, and prayer they did on my behalf.

I must thank my sister, Naomi, who started praying for me after she became a Christian. Her prayers were the foundation of my incredible pilgrimage with Jesus Christ.

Finally my four beautiful children, Alexa, Jayme, Lucas, and Noah, who have become my inspiration in life. I never knew I would be able to love human beings so much. Thank you!

THE LORD'S FINANCIAL PLAN

Gain
Financial Freedom!

A New Beginning

Colossians 3:23, 24:

And whatever you do, do it heartily, as to the Lord and not to men, knowing that from the Lord you will receive the reward of the inheritance; for you serve the Lord Christ.

D o you worry about money? What bills do you pay first? When will the car get fixed? How are you going to finance your children's education? Are you concerned about what would happen to your family should you pass away? What will your lifestyle be like when you retire? Will your family have an inheritance, or will the courts, nursing homes, and the government take most of your estate when you die? Who *doesn't* have financial worries?

This book explains how to develop a practical financial plan from a Biblical perspective that helps you to successfully handle these financial problems now and in the future in accordance with God's will. Because it is the *Lord's* Financial Plan, you can have the confidence of knowing it will be done right.

This is also a book for Christians who desire to be completely surrendered to God's will. Financial stewardship will be discussed and it will bring a whole new way of thinking in your walk with the Lord. It will also change the way you act.

The great purpose of education is not knowledge but action. After reading this book, you will have the knowledge to be able to act in accordance with God's plan with regards to managing your money. The book is divided into three concepts, or three themes. We will learn about the following:

1. Understanding our roles as Financial Stewards.
2. Increasing our ability to Give.
3. Leaving our timeless Legacy.

Each of the three themes is discussed in detail, but with the understanding that they will be incorporated into real monetary financial planning ideas. Financial planning in and of itself is an enormous subject, and I am sorry to say cannot be completely digested in one reading of this or any other book. This particular book is part behavior modification, part Bible study, and part resource manual.

Probably the most difficult concept for anyone to accept, myself included, is that God owns everything and we must relinquish control to Him. Each one of us must first understand our role as a steward (which is discussed in more detail in Chapter Two), in order to get our mindset in the right condition. Almost every previous concept of what we have must change. It is no longer "Mine!" **It always has and always will belong to God.**

Our mentality since we were small children must be altered. We have all heard a child say, "Give it back – it's mine!" Each one of us has probably said this very same thing. The strange aspect to this is the fact that the child says this instinctively; it is not a learned behavior. To the little boy or girl who receives a gift, they innately believe they now own it; it is now "theirs" to do with as they like.

We can help children understand stewardship at an early age, if we explain to them that they need to take care of and share the toy, because it is really God's toy and He entrusted them with it. Trying to correct a youngster in this can be as frustrating as teaching a puppy where to go to the bathroom. But with patience and persistence, the dog finally learns. However, most children never learn this concept of stewardship early and it carries on to adulthood. In the case for stewardship, it really is hard to teach an old dog new tricks. Solomon tells us in Proverbs 22:6 to:

> *Train up a child in the way he should go, and when*
> *he is old he will not depart from it.*

We usually think of this verse for the wayward child, the Prodigal Son, or the Backslider, who will come back to a godly lifestyle after turning away from God. However, this passage is for *all* aspects of bringing up a child in God's method of child rearing. Parents have an awesome responsibility to train and dedicate our children to the Lord, especially in the concept of stewardship.

The earlier we learn stewardship, the better off we will be, because when we get older, the lessons from God can be either a gentle reminder or a harsh rebuke. It is a matter of how much control we want, or how much control we want to give to our Father in Heaven. Who do you think is going to do a better job, us or God?

After we understand our role as a steward and that God owns everything, then another stark reality takes place. God allows us to make money so that we can give it away. God tells us to also give a small portion back to Him as a way of showing our love for Him.

The money we have is really God's. He has given each one of us special gifts and abilities. Some of these abilities allow us to earn an income. If He didn't give us gifts and abilities, we would not be able to earn an income. This is something we must comprehend – God gave us the ability to earn money.

> Deuteronomy 8:18a says, *And you shall remember*
> *the Lord your God, for it is He who gives you*
> *power to get wealth.*

I have worked with some individuals who have had a hard time with this truth. Oh, they agree with what I am saying conceptually, however, deep down they still believe it is *their own* abilities that have generated an income all these years.

Their thought process goes something like this, "I went to school to be in the line of work I am in. I've worked hard and sacrificed to be in my position. And, worst case scenario, I could always work at a fast food restaurant."

But the truth is that God allowed them to be born or placed in an environment where they could get an education. God gave them an opportunity to be interviewed for the job. God entrusted them with the work ethic that has blessed them. Finally, God has even bestowed on them the physical abilities to work, even at a McDonald's restaurant.

Without God's grace to us, we would not and could not make money. We all should be so thankful to God that we should *want* to give some back to Him. But according to The Barna Research Group, it is not so for over 80% of Christians. Less than 20% of evangelical Christians tithe their income to the Lord. It is an interesting phenomenon that those who tithe because they love and trust God have learned they never really miss the amount tithed. Notice, I said with love for God, not with a reluctant or fearful heart.

We will learn about budgeting and how to develop a plan to get out of consumer debt. Budgeting and debt elimination is not a fun exercise and not many people follow through with it, but with determination and faith in God, anybody can do it.

After the initial enthusiasm from starting something new, reality will set in. The disillusionment of this reality is sometimes tougher than the original expectations. The commitment will lower and then confidence in your ability can wither away. My hope is that through steadfast faith in the power of the Holy Spirit, you will stay on the course and not lose heart.

> Gal. 6:9   *And let us not grow weary while doing good, for in due season we shall reap if we do not lose heart.*

There are plenty of resources available already on the subjects of budgeting and getting out of debt, and we won't spend much time on them. Not every person or family needs to keep a budget or has a lot of consumer debt. I do make it very easy and simple, though, and you will read some things you have not read or heard before.

Just realize these are the tools available for anyone who needs them in their financial planning, and it needs to be done early in the process. They are very important in our role as a steward. *The main reason we budget and eliminate debt is so we will have a surplus of money.*

It is so important to understand that we need this extra money

---

Not having a financial plan is like being in a ship without a rudder.

---

to start financial planning and this is why it needs to be done in the beginning. This extra money will be the funding vehicle for our financial planning. We will then talk about what to do with this surplus and how to use it correctly towards The Lord's Financial Plan. We will then begin the practical side of financial planning.

There is a section on how to protect your earning power so that a catastrophe does not destroy your family's hopes and dreams. Another chapter tells where you can invest your money, how to invest appropriately, and *why* we should invest our money (wait until you see what Jesus has to say about investing). A different chapter discusses how to distribute your assets after you pass away. It will explain how to give and to whom we give all that the Lord gave us, in the best way.

On a side note, our giving doesn't always involve money. The Lord also wants some of the time and talents He gave us, as well as the treasure.

The more we give, the more the Lord gives back to us, and then the more we are able to give, and then the Lord blesses us even more, and then we can give more, and then... Can you see how perfect God's system is? Our Father in Heaven is willing and wants to bless His obedient children.

Finally, we will explain leaving a legacy that lasts *forever*. Only two things have eternal ramifications and they are God's Word and a life changed because of Jesus Christ. A person who gives his life to Jesus on earth will live with Jesus in Heaven for all eternity. Nothing else lasts forever, except God's Word, and we have no control of this part since it is already written.

But we can help direct people to Jesus Christ with the everlasting legacy we leave behind. Nothing else is more important than winning souls for Jesus. For example, the great philanthropists who have been honored with monuments in their name – these monuments will eventually decay. The talented novelists – their writings will in time decompose. Gifted composers – their music will stop playing some day.

However, the work of an evangelist, teacher, speaker, missionary, and pastor funded by obedient Christians, will last for all eternity. Leaving a legacy that lasts forever is a vital aspect in The Lord's Financial Plan. You will learn about the available techniques to leave a legacy. This is not just for the wealthy. It is for all walks of life. Remember Jesus talking about a poor widow putting in two mites? She put in the entire livelihood that she had, and she will be remembered forever, because it is in God's Word.

These three themes:

1) Understanding our roles as Financial Stewards
2) Increasing our ability to Give, and
3) Leaving a timeless Legacy

will be incorporated into the vast world of true and practical financial planning. Because what would it help to change our attitude and not know the financial tools available to be an effective steward in today's financial structure? Not very much.

The financial planning procedures can be intimidating if not explained properly, especially for someone just starting out. Consequently, I have tried to keep it simple and easy for the novice to understand.

This reminds me of my thinking last year when I was trying to comprehend the enormous college planning process for my oldest daughter, Alexa. I recall saying; "There is no way I can learn all the necessary stuff to do it right." Then I went to her high school's college planning prep course for two hours, looked at the recommended websites, and read most of the materials they gave out.

Now I understand the procedures in applying for college, the people to see, and what papers to fill out. It is not nearly as horrifying as I previously imagined, and neither will financial planning be. Some basic knowledge has made me comfortable and confident that my daughter will be able to go to the college of her choice. (We found out *today* that she was accepted to Westmont College in Montecito, California!)

You will feel the same way about financial planning after reading this book. You can have confidence that your family's financial plan is going in the right direction, is based on Biblical principals, and that God will honor and bless you because of it.

I will break the financial planning process down to basic levels, and it too will be in three sections. The first section is *Protection*, the second section is *Accumulation*, and the last section is called *Preservation*. You will know for sure that your family will be taken care of if anything disastrous should happen to you (Protection). You will have a good idea of what your retirement will look like (Accumulation). Lastly, you will know where all your assets will go after you pass away (Preservation).

Financial planning is not a one-time event. It is an on-going work in progress, just like we are to our Father in Heaven. It can take several months or even years to get your financial house in order. But after it is set up correctly, your stewardship responsibility lies only in the maintenance of keeping it in order and up-to-date.

> Phil. 1:6, *Being confident in this very thing, that He who has begun a good work in you will complete it until the day of Jesus Christ.*

Stewardship

Mathew 6:33

But seek first the kingdom of God and His righteous-
ness, and all these things shall be added to you.

To fully appreciate a book about the Lord's Financial Plan, we must understand our basic or fundamental core belief. To do this we must start at the first verse in the Bible (No, we are not going to begin here and continue through to Revelations, but we must start here).

> Gen 1:1, *In the beginning God created the Heavens*
> *and the Earth.*

Because God *created,* that makes Him a *creator.* Moreover, God is *the* creator. He created time and space, day and night, Heaven and earth, water and land, sun and moon, and food and animals. Since God created everything, He then is the *owner* of everything.

Other synonyms for this word "creator" are architect, author, mastermind, designer, engineer, and planner. For example, an engineer designs a bridge to go over a river and it is "his" design because he created it. An author writes a short story and it is "his" story. An architect plans a room addition and it is "his" plans. They can sell them, use them, or throw them away, because they own them. These examples show that the owner can do what he wants with their creations, because they are theirs.

God owns every*thing* but what about every*body*? It says a few verses later in Genesis that God made every man and woman as well.

Gen. 1:27, *God created man in His own image; in the image of God He created him; male and female He created them.*

So then we are His, and God owns us because He made each one of us. God even spent extra time creating us. Where He *spoke* all the animals into existence, He *formed* man, Adam, with the dust of the ground and then God breathed into Adam's nostrils and gave him the breath of life.

Each one of us is exclusively unique. There has never been an individual just like you before, and there will never be anyone exactly like you in the future. We have our own fingerprints, DNA, abilities, likes, style, looks, personality, gifts, and dreams.

It is actually mind-boggling when one thinks of how many different people God has created already. There are approximately six billion people on this planet who are alive now and an estimated six billion men and women who have already lived and died on Earth since Adam and Eve were in existence (give or take a dozen). Each person is personally known and was created in the Lord's mind before the foundation of the world began.

Just think about how creative our God is. Besides the 12 billion human beings He has made, the world has so many animals that no one could possibly count them. No one even knows how many *kinds* there are. According to the World Book encyclopedia, scientists have classified or grouped almost a million kinds of animals. But every year they discover hundreds of new ones. Of these, more than 800,000 groups are insects (Yuck!).

There are more than 30,000 species of fish and about 9000 different kinds of birds. Yet, scientists believe there could possibly be more than 10 million forms of life yet to be discovered.

Many of us take plants for granted, but without them there could not be life on earth. Plants create the food that all the animals eat, so we are using the food that plants make whenever we eat a steak or drink a glass of milk. Scientists know there are more than 335,000 different species of plants.

We are to glorify God with everything He has entrusted us with.

This is just life on earth, not to mention the vastness of the universe and the millions or possibly billions of galaxies. Alternatively, think about the microscopic atom that still has unlimited discoveries left in it. Our human mind is not able to comprehend the incredible genius of God. But then again, if we were able to figure out God, He would not be worthy of all our praise. With all our breathtaking discoveries of modern technology, *if* we were ever to figure out everything He had designed up through yesterday, there would already be more new ones we don't know today.

> Eccl. 3:11, *He has made every thing beautiful in its time. Also He has put eternity in their heart, except that no one can find out the work that God does from beginning to the end.*

Okay, since God is the creator and we are His creation, what then is our responsibility or our role here on earth? The answer is we are to glorify God with everything He has entrusted us with. This is called being a *steward.*

In other words, we *manage* what God has given us. God is the owner and we are His stewards of *everything* He has bestowed on us. This would be all tangible *and* intangible items, including all of our gifts, talents, education, time, relationships, careers, family, friends, emotions, and all material possessions. We are simply managing these for God while we are living this side of Heaven. He has created us for the purpose of glorifying Him and we do this by being the best stewards we can be.

According to Webster, the word *stewardship* means the individual's responsibility to manage his life and property with proper regard to the rights of others. If we think what we possess is ours, and forget who really owns it, then we will get ourselves into trouble. Most people will say, "My car," "My apartment," "My children," and "My job." Very seldom do we hear, "The house the Lord has allowed me to stay in for now, all the while taking care of it for Him and His glory."

Most people think the items they have in their possession are their own property. The Bible says differently, though.

> In Haggai 2:8 the prophet of God says, *"The silver is mine, and the gold is mine" says the Lord of hosts.*

> In Psalms 24 1:1, a Psalm of David, says, *The earth is the Lord's, and all its fullness, the world and those who dwell therein.*

People don't know, or never realized, or ignore, or forgot that everything is God's and they are the steward of what He has entrusted to them. The one item that people take the most ownership of is money. "I've worked for it, I earned it, it's mine and I will do with it as I like" is a lot of people's attitude.

If we refuse to acknowledge the fact that the Lord owns all the wealth, too, then we will *never* experience God's will and His blessings for our finances. As a consequence, our lives will be characterized constantly by anxiety in the area of money.

People's negative attitude about their responsibility and stewardship of money is understandable. It makes people uncomfortable talking about their financial situation. We have been taught it is impolite to ask others about their earnings and debts since we were young.

How many times have you heard a child say to someone, "Wow! That's cool, how much was it?"

Then they get rebuked by their parent, "Don't ask that — it's rude!"

However, we can have the false assurance that our possessions will speak louder than our words. "You won't know how much I make, but you'll have an idea by – where I live, the car I drive, and the vacations I take."

Talking about money in the church is even harder for a pastor, especially the modern church in America. There have been blatant cases of misuse in the receiving of gifts and donations in a few ministries in the last couple of decades. People are hesitant to give and pastors are hesitant to talk about gifting partly because of a few bad examples.

Those irresponsible receivers of gifts and donations will have to answer to God for their sin someday. However, their wrong does not excuse anyone else from their own responsibility to give.

Rom. 14:12, *So then each of us shall give an account of himself to God.*

A middle-aged woman was overheard saying in the lobby of her church, "I don't like hearing our pastor talk about giving, tithing, and money in church. It just kills the spirit!" If it did, the only spirit it kills is the spirit of the flesh.

Another reason pastors are reluctant to discuss the topic of stewardship is because they do not want to scare away any visitors, and the subject does sometimes. I remember a time right after I surrendered my life to Jesus and was attending a small church.

I was full of zeal and invited everyone I knew to come to church with my family and me. Do you remember those days? I was talking to a young lady who was a customer of mine at the time, when she mentioned she was looking for a church to call home and it had been a long search. I could tell she was frustrated. I told her how alive and exciting my church was and I thought she'd love it. This small church I attended at the time had a real good children's program, a wonderful worship leader, and the pastor was an awesome Bible teacher.

She brought her whole family to my church the next Sunday and I was excited to see her. The pastor, who had never spoken of money, giving, or tithing in my previous 12 months of attending, decided this was the time. Because the topic of stewardship is so wide and there was so much to go over, the pastor preached longer than usual. He spoke for an hour and a half on this subject, thirty minutes over his normal time, and he still wasn't able to give this important Biblical principal justice. After we finally got out, my friends had already left – never to be seen again.

That was a case like the old joke about a Midwest town that was in the middle of a terrible blizzard. Only the pastor and one member, a dairyman, showed up for church on Sunday. The pastor asked the dairyman if he still wanted to hear his prepared sermon. The member said he was there already and yes, to go ahead. After the service, the pastor asked the dairyman what he thought of the sermon. He answered, "Pastor, when I go out to feed the cows and only one cow shows up – I don't go and drop the whole load on him!"

In churches today, we do not teach enough about financial stewardship. Pastors should not try to teach this subject once a year, timidly and with trepidation just to get it over with, and expect their flock to comprehend the importance. It should be done in a series of sermons and with gentleness and grace.

Churches that go through the Bible in a verse by verse format, one book or one letter at a time, cannot help but talk about money and giving, because the Bible is full of scriptures discussing the important topic of stewardship. I know of several churches that do this and of course, they are full of Christians who understand stewardship and the role they have been given by God. These churches are thriving in several ministries because they have the funds to implement incredible life-changing programs. And at the same time, the courageous pastors of these churches are paid accordingly, as they should be.

I am going to go on a little tangent for a moment. Pastors shouldn't have to worry about whether or not they can take care of their own families financially while taking care of their church family spiritually. Please understand, I'm not suggesting that pastors should live extravagantly, but they deserve adequate compensation.

A pastor's compensation depends on many factors that have to be considered. For example, the church's financial resources, the pastor's experience, education, and years of faithful service, and the compensation paid by other churches that are similar in size, which is based on average church attendance and budget. The apostle Paul understood this problem and addressed it.

> 1 Timothy 5:17, 18 says, *Let the elders who rule well be counted worthy of double honor, especially those who labor in the word and doctrine. For the Scripture says, "You shall not muzzle an ox while it treads out the grain," and, "The laborer is worthy of his wages."*

Consider for a moment how difficult the job of a pastor is. He has to go through extensive schooling, so he can teach God's Word in a way that a non-Christian will be affected enough to want to know more about the Lord, and still provide nourishment for a life-long student of the Bible.

The pastor must have some training on counseling issues ranging from pornography addiction to parenting challenges. He has to be an effective leader in his home, community, and the church staff, so people will want to follow him.

Add to this, the pastor's incredible burden for his "flock" and his responsibility to them, and the toll this takes on his own family. And of course the impossible task of trying to please everyone from the trustees to the nursery helpers. Also, can you imagine the spiritual warfare that must constantly plague the pastors? They are serving the Lord usually seven days a week and Satan is continuously attacking them because of this service.

God has chosen, anointed, and set aside pastors so they would be equipped to be the shepherds of the flock. They need time to study God's Word, pray for the church, and show themselves worthy of God's call. That is a full-time position and should be compensated as such.

Is it any wonder that Paul talked about the pay to leaders of the church a couple of times? He was starting churches everywhere and he would have to build up pastors to lead them and then he would go to the next town to start over again. He needed pastors who could devote their whole lives to this new faith and still be able to support their own families. Paul, talking to the new church in Corinth, says in 1 Cor. 9:7:

> *Who ever goes to war at his own expense? Who plants a vineyard and does not eat of its fruit? Or who tends a flock and does not drink of the milk of the flock?*
> Skipping to verse 11, *If we have sown spiritual things for you, is it a great thing if we reap your material things? If others are partakers of this right over you, are we not even more? Nevertheless we have not used this right, but endure all things lest we hinder the gospel of Christ. Do you not know that those who minister the holy things eat of the things of the temple, and those who serve at the altar partake of the offerings of the altar? Even so the Lord has commanded that those that preach the gospel*

should live from the gospel.

Part of *our* stewardship to the pastors is to support them financially, edify them spiritually, and encourage them practically. It is extremely difficult for pastors to talk on some subjects God wants them to preach on, because of the backlash they might receive. Pastors need the reassurance from their church that it is OK to talk about painful topics, including financial stewardship.

But, if the pastors are not going to talk about financial stewardship, then somebody better start talking about it, because if you look at the statistics of the Christian compared to the unbeliever, you will be shocked. Christians have the same divorce rate of 50% of first year marriages, and financial problems account for 70% of these divorces. We have just as much consumer debt as the secular world. We are caught up in the devil's trap of materialism and consumerism and want what the world has to offer just like everyone else. Christians are no different in the way we handle money than people who do not have the Bible as their guide. Most Christians are not good witnesses when it comes to their finances.

Any church leader will tell you the 80/20 rule applies in giving and serving, that is, 20% of Christians are supporting the church and 80% are receiving from the church. Obviously this generality does not apply to every church; however, less than 15% are actually tithing on their income.

I read once where if the entire Christian population tithed the minimum of 10%, the world hunger, the homeless, and the basic medical needs of the world would be taken care of in 6 - 8 months. I'm not sure how accurate this is, but consider what the church is able to accomplish with less than 15% tithing and what could be done with the additional 85%. Add the Power of the Holy Spirit working exponentially with all this obedient living, and the church could do even more miraculous things.

I believe we need to talk more about money, finances, and possessions in churches. The Bible has over 2000 verses regarding money. Two-thirds of Jesus' parables dealt with money, posses-sions, and stewardship. The Lord spoke so much about it because He knows how important it is. We cannot separate God and our money. Jesus said where your money is, that is where your heart is. The Bible, "Basic Instructions Before Leaving Earth," tells us everything we need to know about stewardship, giving, and finan-cial planning.

Christians need to comprehend how important this concept of stewardship is. It is the running theme throughout this book and my hope is that it will become a running theme in your life. The first step to take is to transfer ownership back to God, since it is His

---

The first step is to transfer ownership back to God, since it is His already

---

already. The Lord gives us all the abilities, gifts, skills, time, edu-cation, jobs, and anything else we need to be good stewards of what He has entrusted us with. We just need to surrender these attributes back to God so He can guide and lead us.

However, if *we* take ownership, then *we* take responsibility and then we become irresponsible. We then do things *we* think *we* should do. This will invariably get us into financial trouble. We will then mismanage God's money. We will do this by getting into too much consumer debt, buying on impulse, misusing credit, or taking on too much risk.

When we get into trouble, we will do anything to fix it. We will work two jobs and then not be home for the family, or not be able to serve the Lord because of not being able to schedule it in. Even worse are the cases when the spouse has to go to work when they might not have wanted to in the first place.

We will try to earn money by "investing" to get a very high rate of return or taking part in get-rich-quick schemes. Usually these plans are not the Lord's plans so they will invariably fail. Not only do people fail in trying to fix their financial problems by themselves, they can bring additional stress to the already taxed family. Not to mention the health problems all this causes from lack of rest by working and worrying too much.

So what should our attitude about money and wealth be? God is the owner, we are His stewards, and God entrusts us with the ability to earn money. The creation of an income is both a gift and a talent to us from the Lord. God is not interested in our aptitude, but our attitude.

The correct attitude is to seek God's will and purpose for what He has given to us and entrusted to us. There is absolutely nothing wrong with asking God for wisdom, guidance, and direction regarding our money. It is wrong, however, to go our own way and then expect the Lord to bail us out every time.

The Lord has many uses for money in our lives. God can use money to *strengthen* our trust in Him, *if* we will accept our roles as stewards and turn our finances over to Him. God will sometimes use money to *measure* our trustworthiness. If we cannot be trusted with small things, will He be able to entrust us with bigger things? Finally, God can use money to *prove* His love to us by supplying all our needs. Always our *needs*, but not always *our* wants and greeds.

To achieve the Lord's best, we must apply what He says. It will not help you to just read this book for information and then not do any of the applications. It will be an exercise in frustration to know and not do, especially as you get older in years or mature in your walk with Jesus. Have you ever heard the saying, "Information without application leads to frustration"? Frustration is doing the same thing over and over and expecting different results.

The first item on the to-do list then is, to transfer ownership back to God where it belongs. If you have never verbalized to God this transfer of ownership, here is a prayer I'd suggest saying before reading any further:

Dear Heavenly Father,

I know you are the creator of all and own everything. Sometimes I forget this fact and I ask for your forgiveness. I am sorry for trying to do it my way and not trusting you completely. I transfer all tangible and intangible gifts back to you. I am asking for wisdom, direction, and the right attitude regarding my financial stewardship. Thank you for hearing and answering this prayer. I ask this in the name of Jesus. Amen.

One incredible lesson I have learned over the years is that God *wants* to bless His children abundantly! Christians are heirs to the throne, adopted into God's family. We have the Power of the Holy Spirit living inside us.

We human beings, with our limited knowledge, can only see or want what we think is *good* for us. God with His unlimited wisdom and love, knows what is *best* for us. Our mindset must change.

We need to expect God to do amazing things through us, by faith and obedience, including our finances. We should be willing to let the Lord handle our lives according to *His* will and wait until we see the absolutely remarkable blessings that will come to us.

We have not because we ask not, according to Jesus. Surrender everything to God and let the creator of all do His work in us and see if you can contain all the joy that will come!

Job 36:11 *If they obey and serve Him, they shall spend their days in prosperity and their years in pleasures.*

Chapter 2 – Stewardship
Review Points

- We are stewards, or managers, of everything tangible and intangible that God has entrusted to us.

- Part of our stewardship includes supporting and edifying our pastors.

- Transferring ownership back to God where it belongs is the first step to proper stewardship.

- Prepare yourself for an amazing adventure with the Lord.

Tithing

Deuteronomy 26:16, 17

This day the Lord your God commands you to observe these statutes and judgements; therefore you shall be careful to observe them with all your heart and with all your soul. Today you have proclaimed the Lord to be your God, and that you will walk in His ways and keep His statutes, His commandments, and His judgements, and that you will obey His voice.

After acknowledging God is the owner and we are His stewards of everything He has entrusted to us, comes an integral part of the Lord's Financial Plan. That is the concept of tithing. Unfortunately, tithing has become a controversial subject and it shouldn't be because it is evident in the Bible that we are supposed to tithe. In this chapter we will explain what tithing is, the history of tithing, what Jesus says about tithing, and the promised blessings for tithing.

The word *tithe* means literally "a tenth" and God commands us to tithe, or give 10% of our first fruits.

Exodus 22:29a *You shall not delay to offer the first of your ripe produce and your juices.*

Exodus 23:19a *The first of the firstfruits of your land you shall bring into the house of the Lord your God.*

This is 10% of *gross* income that comes to us, not 10% *net* income, and not 10% of what is left after we pay everyone else. There is a huge difference between first fruits and leftovers. We don't *give* our tithes to God; we *pay* our tithes. This is God's commanded small portion back to Him for all that He has given to us to manage for Him. This can be uncomfortable and difficult to a lot of people.

You may be thinking, "How in the world can I pay 10% to God when I am barely making it now?" That is a fair question. Let me ask you something. What if you didn't pay your taxes? What if

---

There is a huge difference between first fruits and leftovers.

---

you didn't pay your rent or mortgage? Insurance premiums? Utilities? Car payment? You would lose the privilege of using these necessary items. By not giving back to the Lord what is already His, you lose the privilege of God's blessings and protection.

Tithing is a form of worship. Tithing is an expression of our love to our Lord. When you pay your tithes, it shows God how much you trust in His faithfulness to provide for you and your family.

I love how my pastor asks for the offering during our praise and worship time. This is the best time to give, because as we are praising our Lord with our mouths, hands, and instruments, we can also praise and worship Him with our checkbooks.

Unfortunately, this is an overlooked aspect of worship in many churches. Several churches do not even mention tithing and giving during the service and have offering boxes outside of the sanctuary. They have forgotten that it is as much a part of our worship to the Lord as singing a hymn or praying a prayer.

As a result of this, many churches have lost the joy they should have when they bring in their tithing. When the leaders of the church minimize the importance of tithing, then the congregation doesn't understand its importance. The speed of the leader is the speed of the group.

It is interesting to know the history of the tithe. It began with Abram in the book of Genesis, even before he became known as Abraham, when he gave a tithe to Melchizedek who was the king of Salem and also a priest of God.

Abram had just rescued his nephew Lot after a major battle in Sodom and Gomorrah when Melchizedek came out to meet him. Melchizedek blessed Abram and in return, Abram gave him a tithe of all he possessed. In this case, Abram gave 10% of his whole estate. Abram gave out of the kindness of his heart; there wasn't a rule suggesting he give this amount. The actual law of tithing came much later.

By the way, Melchizedek is one of the most mysterious figures in the Bible. Melchizedek means the King of Peace and the King of Righteousness. Melchizedek had no beginning and no end but was like the Son of God and he remains a priest continually, according to the scriptures. This describes our Savior Jesus Christ.

It is believed that Melchizedek was a "Christophony," an appearance of the preincarnate Christ, before Jesus was born here on earth. Hebrews 7:1-10 in the New Testament explains all of this. Because Abram paid him tithes illustrates how great Melchizedek was. The fact that Melchizedek blessed Abram establishes Melchizedek's superiority, because the greater always blesses the inferior according to Hebrews 7:7.

The concept of tithing was so important to God that He instituted it hundreds of years before Moses. Abraham has been called the father of the faith, and was justified by his faith. If Abraham practiced tithing when he saw Christ through faith, how can we who have Christ living in us, do less?

Abraham's grandson, Jacob, made a vow to the Lord regarding tithing 300 years before the Mosaic Law. Undoubtedly the story had been passed down from generation to generation of how God had previously blessed Abraham and Isaac.

> Genesis 28:20-22 *Then Jacob made a vow, saying, "If God will be with me, and keep me in this way that I am going, and give me bread to eat and clothing to put on, so that I come back to my father's house in peace, then the Lord shall be my God. And this stone which I have set as a pillar shall be God's house, and of all that You give I will surely give a tenth to you.*

This vow to God was a sign of genuine devotion. God did honor this vow to Jacob when we read farther in Genesis. God changed Jacob's name to Israel and had twelve sons who established the twelve tribes of Israel. Incidentally, Jacob also became incredibly wealthy.

Three hundred years after this, Moses wrote the Law and it includes the rules of tithing. The Israelites were in an agricultural society, so no money is mentioned. They traded and bartered, and did business with grain, oils, and livestock.

The Lord commanded the first fruits of all increase to be given to the Levites, who were in charge of the temple and offerings to the Lord. The Levites lived off the tithe just as our church leaders do today. At the time of Moses, the tithing was actually more than 10%. It was well above that when you add all the extra amounts to the temple, such as the offerings to the Levites every 3 years, Jubilee, and the Heave Offerings.

Some people might say that is all well and good, however, that is the Old Testament law and I have been freed from the law because of what Jesus did on the cross for me. And that is exactly what it says in the New Testament.

> Rom. 7:6 *But now we have been delivered from the law, having died to what we were held by, so that we*

should serve in the newness of the Spirit and not in
the oldness of the letter.

I agree that we are free from the law and live by grace, but this freedom assumes *new and greater* responsibilities for the one who is liberated from the law, the Christian. The law no longer rules the believer. God's Holy Spirit rules in his heart and the believer's responsibilities are more profound as a result. Jesus mentions tithing in Math 23:23 and Luke 11:42 and they are parallel passages. We will look at what it says in Luke.

Jesus says, *"But woe to you Pharisees! For you*
tithe mint and rue and all manner of herbs, and pass
by judgement and the love of God. These you ought
to have done, without leaving the others undone."

Jesus rebukes the scribes and Pharisees not for tithing, which they did to the letter of the Law, even to the point of counting out the grain and spices, but for not exhibiting justice, mercy, and faith. Jesus is saying they should be more merciful, kind, and loving, and still continue to tithe.

Jesus always magnified living by grace than by living by the law. He demonstrated the difference between the righteousness of the new believer and the righteousness of the scribes and Pharisees. He elevated our responsibilities in every way including anger, lust, divorce, oaths, and love for our enemies. It makes sense then that there would be no less grace in the area of tithing. A tithe, or 10%, is the *starting point* in our giving to the Lord. I like to say that Abram commenced it, Moses commanded it, and Jesus commended it.

Jesus speaks of tithing only this one time, Luke 11:42 and Mathew 23:23 and they are basically the same passage. Because He only said it once does not lessen its truth or importance. It is significant to point out that Jesus said only once, "You must be born again" and that was only to one person, Nicodemus, late at night. His approval and exhortation to tithe ought to be sufficient motivation for any Christian.

The apostle Paul doesn't specifically mention tithing in the early church. He does talk of giving on a weekly basis, though.

> 1 Cor. 16:2 *On the first day of the week let each one of you lay something aside, storing up as he may prosper, that there be no collections when I come.*

One possible reason Paul did not elaborate on tithing is that the early church was already faithfully keeping the law of the tithe. In fact, the early church sold *all* their possessions and gave it to the apostles to distribute to the needy. They gave all! The church had a communal style of living back then. As the church progressed and grew, this method wasn't practical anymore.

But in the beginning of the church, they lived in fear of persecution and death by the Jewish leaders. The Christians were glad to live together because of the protection this provided. Later when the circumstances changed, they moved back into their own homes and the communal system was abandoned. As long as they were living together they gave *everything* they had.

The first time I heard about tithing was shortly after I came to know Jesus as my Lord and Savior. My wife wanted nothing to do with church at the time, so it was my two daughters and me going every Sunday to a small church. When the offering plate went by, I'd throw a $20.00 bill in there, thinking I was really a giver. I'd look around and say, "How many others are giving $80 – $100 a month?"

With all my pride and arrogance, I thought I was pretty special. My wife knew nothing about this part of church. It was my little secret.

One Sunday, the pastor had a guest speaker, a wonderful older

Christian lady named Christal Clayton, who spoke on giving and tithing. That was the first time I had heard about tithing, let alone this 10% of *gross* income business.

During this time in my life I was a modestly successful small businessman who owned small food markets and delicatessens with a partner, and earned a nice income with all the additional perks and benefits of owning small businesses.

When Christal said the Lord commands 10% of gross income, my first thought was, "How am I going to hide that from my wife?" Starting that next week, however, I started to tithe correctly and haven't stopped since. You get to a point where you are afraid not to tithe, not out of fear of the wrath of God, but because of all the blessings God provides.

Many believers claim the passages of Proverbs 3:5, 6 as their life verses. In fact, they were the first two verses I memorized in the Bible, and in a way they have become my life verses.

> *Trust in the Lord with all your heart, and lean not on your own understanding; In all your ways acknowledge Him, and He will direct your paths.*

But, I think verses 9 and 10 of the same chapter should also become one of our cherished passages to memorize. What an amazing promise from God!

> *Honor the Lord with your possessions, and with the firstfruits of all your increase; So your barns will be filled with plenty, and your vats will overflow with new wine.*

This is how the Lord blesses His people. Luke 6:38 says if you give, it will be given to you, pressed down and running over. You know how in a box of cereal that there is so much air in the package because of shipping and the cereal is now packed down and it is not full anymore? Well, the Lord packs His blessings and then shakes it to get the air out and then refills His blessings so they overflow. No box can contain all that the Lord has for us.

Shortly after I started to tithe the correct amount, things started to go my way financially. I have always been interested in the stock market and started investing at an early age. One day I got a call from your typical New Jersey sounding stockbroker, and I would routinely receive ten of these calls a week, but this time I listened to what he had to say and didn't hang up on him.

Coincidentally, I was reading a couple of stock investing books at the time and what he was saying was what these books were saying I should do when investing in individual stocks. I ended up opening an account with $5000 and he gave me a margin account, which means I was really investing $10,000. Now the second $5000 I was *borrowing* from his brokerage at a 7% interest rate.

All of this money went into one stock that was a huge conglomerate that was supposed to be broken up into little companies if approved by the shareholders. Because of the anticipation of this possibility, the stock was going up like crazy. In two weeks my $5000 was now worth $18,000.

The stockbroker called me again and told me about an IPO, an initial public offering, of a new food company. If I knew nothing else, I knew food companies and it sounded very promising. He got me in this "deal" on Wednesday at $4 a share, Thursday it went public, Friday the stock was worth $12 a share. I cashed out on everything and paid off my margin account, much to the chagrin of the guy from New Jersey and I netted over $30,000 in one month. I'd never made that much money so fast before, and this was before the Dot Com Bubble period.

I made a couple of other quick deals and was making a lot of extra money. Boy did I think I was the dealmaker! "God is really blessing me! This tithing stuff really works! I wish I'd known about this sooner! Everybody should tithe! What an awesome investment God is! If I give more to God, will He give *me* even more?"

My mindset was to give so I can get. I would pray over my tithing check asking God to bless *me* with this money I'm giving. I was a new immature Christian and didn't know any better at the time. Twelve years later and a couple of small fortunes lost, my prayer is now, "Please, Father, use this tithe money for *Your* glory."

There is only one place in the Bible where God says to test Him and His promises to see if He will be faithful, and that is in the small book of Malachi, the last book of the Old Testament. Malachi was a prophet from God to the people of Israel. He was the last voice of God until John the Baptist came onto the scene over 400 years later.

The Israelites were struggling in every area of life at that time of Malachi. They had fallen in sin by marrying pagan men and women, worshipping idols, and then blaming God for their troubles. God uses Malachi to answer the people's complaints about Him, what the Israelites could do about it, and how God will reward them for being so faithful.

> Mal. 3:8-12 *"Will a man rob God? Yet you have robbed Me! But you say, 'In what way have we robbed you?' In tithes and offerings. You are cursed with a curse, for you have robbed Me, even this whole nation. Bring all the tithes into the storehouse, that there may be food in My house, and try Me now in this," says the Lord of Hosts. "If I will not open for you the windows of Heaven and pour out such blessing that there will not be room enough to receive it. And I will rebuke the devourer for your sakes, so that he will not destroy the fruit of your ground, nor shall the vine fail to bear fruit for you in the field," says the Lord of Hosts; "and all nations will call you blessed, for you will be a*

delightful land," says the Lord of Hosts.

I cannot imagine anybody reaching in and taking money out of the offering plate when it comes by, but that is what the Lord is saying if you do not tithe. *"You are robbing Me."* It is His, not ours. It is hard to imagine that we are ripping off our Lord by not giving to Him what is rightfully His to begin with. But that is what the scriptures say.

The whole nation will be cursed for not tithing. One can notice the United States and its giving in our churches. Giving is in a decline and the blessings are getting fewer. Our nation has seen pornography problems increase, crime going up, poverty numbers are up, drug use up, terrorist threats, more floodings, hurricanes, and earthquakes.

Our country was founded on Christian principles and we have been an incredibly blessed nation. However, since the 1960's when we took God out of the schools and courts we have seen a moral decline. Less people believing in Jesus, means less people in church, which means less tithing and giving.

But even the people going to church are not tithing. In 2001, according to the Barna Research Group, 14% of Born Again Christians tithed accordingly. It dropped to 6% in 2002. It did go up in 2003 to 17%, but this still means that over 80% of Christians did not tithe correctly. The annual average dollar amount given to churches by evangelical Christians was only $1411 for the year in 2003. We are following in the footsteps of the Israelites in Malachi's time of seeing a moral and spiritual decline.

In verse 10 it says to *bring all the tithes to the storehouse.* The storehouse is the church. This would be your home church or church where you fellowship the most.

If you are a "shut-in" and cannot physically attend a church, I suggest you find a good Bible teaching ministry on television or radio and send them your tithe, because that would be considered your home church. The church where you get fed the Word of God is where all your tithing goes. You shouldn't send it to another ministry that you feel needs the money more. That would be like going to one grocery store to buy your food and then paying for it at another store you think could really use the money.

That there would be food in My house, means spiritual food as well as physical nourishment for the congregation and their ministries. The physical food is for the hungry, homeless, and needy. This food is bought with tithing money to fill the pantries of churches to give away as needed. The spiritual food is the Word of God preached in churches. We get "fed" by the message from the pastors. Churches are run by the tithes that come in. Tithing pays for the ministries, pastors, staff, and miscellaneous expenses.

As stated earlier, the only place in the Bible where God challenges people to test Him in His faithfulness is in verse 10. He never challenges us in prayer, faith, love, parenting, or marriage, only in our tithing. And His blessings will be so much we cannot even receive it all!

These blessings will not always mean financial blessings, though. The blessings from God are also a source of protection for us. *God will rebuke the devourer for your sakes.* The Israelites, as agriculturists or farmers, made their living by the "fruit" of the ground. God watched over their fields and they would be protected from insects and bad weather when they tithed. He rebuked the devourer in the ground and in the air.

God will protect us from our devourer, Satan, night and day as well. The devil searches people he can destroy and devour, but the Lord Himself protects us by saying in essence, "Get behind Me, Satan, and leave My child alone!" However you make a living, God wants to bless you. These blessings will not always be tangible, they can be intangible, also. The blessings could be joy in your work, respect from your colleagues, or incredible fulfillment in a rewarding career.

If the church were obedient to the command of tithing, other people would see the incredible grace God has bestowed on us. It would be an example, or a representation of His kindness to the whole world. God's blessings are always in reserve for His children who are teachable and obedient.

I love how Malachi 3:8-10 reads in the Living Bible:

> *"Will a man rob God? Surely not! And yet you have robbed me. 'What do you mean? When did we ever rob you?' You have robbed me of the tithes and offerings due to me. And so the awesome curse of God is cursing you, for your whole nation has been robbing me. Bring all the tithes into the storehouse so that there will be food enough in my Temple; if you do, I will open up the windows of Heaven for you and pour out a blessing so great you won't have room enough to take it in! Try it! Let me prove it to you!"*

God is almost pleading with us to trust Him. He cannot make it any plainer to us.

God doesn't have us tithe to raise cash; He does it to raise kids, His kids. He wants us to be more like Him. God is a giver – He gave us everything we need: life, grace, mercy, forgiveness, sustenance, and salvation. He has given this to us FREE! He just wants us to give the same portion – 10% – rich or poor.

The sacrifice is the same for everyone. Can you possibly think of a better way? Of course not. Tithing should be considered a privilege and not a command. God could have established a thousand different ways to carry out His work, but that would have deprived us of the blessings that flow back to us.

There are too many stories to tell to prove God's amazing grace on people who give to the Lord. There have been numerous times in my life, since I became a Christian, when God provided just enough for that day, week, or month. If I would think rationally, it just does not make sense.

One time in the midst of the worst time in my life financially, we were down to the last $100 in December with no idea where the next dollar was coming from, when my wife won $2000 at a grocery store! That was the best Christmas we ever had.

On Christmas Eve a few weeks later, I got a job as a food salesman for a cheese and bakery company. What makes this so remarkable is that food companies are the busiest during the Christmas holiday and the last thing in the world they have time for is to hire and train someone during that period, but that is exactly what they did.

We were faithful when we tithed on the $2000 and of course God was faithful, and provided a great job and good income for a few years. During this time at the food company, a very successful financial advisor introduced me to the financial industry and I left the food world after 20 years and started a new exciting career as a financial planner.

Many people are confused about the difference between offerings and tithing. Offerings are different than tithes. We give offerings *after* we have tithed to our church. This you may give anywhere the Lord leads you. It could be a different ministry you believe in or a handout to someone in need. It is a mistake to think giving money to a person is part of your tithe.

People often ask me about a spouse who is not a Believer and how to deal with the situation. To the "natural" person, tithing does not make any sense at all. They are spiritually "blind" and are unable to comprehend the truth, and the scriptures appear foolish to them.

> 1 Cor. 2:14 *But the natural man does not receive the things of the Spirit of God, for they are foolishness to him; nor can he know them, because they are spiritually discerned.*

I tell them the non-believing spouse is not expected to understand spiritual matters any more than a non-baseball fan is expected to understand the infield fly rule. But you, knowing the Truth, are to be obedient to the Word.

Whatever income comes to you, whether it is from your job or your "allowance," then you are responsible to tithe. God will honor your faithfulness and will bless you. As a witness for God, make sure your spouse realizes where all the blessings are coming from. Try it and let God prove it to you!

Just for fun, I've listed household names that believed in our Lord and the tithing principle. J.C. Penny, original owner of the department store, J.L. Kraft of Kraft Cheese, Henry Heinz of Heinz 57, William Proctor of Proctor and Gamble, and Milton Hershey of Hershey's Chocolate. There's also Will Keith Kellogg of Kellogg's cereal, Marquis Converse of Converse shoes, and William Dodge of the Dodge automobile. Of course, there are many others, but it is interesting to note these name brands that benefited from God's amazing blessings on them and the awesome witnesses they have been throughout the years.

I confess that many people think I am too legalistic regarding the tithe, and that tithing itself is legalistic. But why did Abraham and Jacob give a tenth of all they had before any law? I try my best to do what the Bible says to do. Tithing is a means of acknowledging God is the owner of everything and we are mere stewards. God wants us to be obedient and to live by faith. Tithing is faith in action. The Body of Christ is God's family, and if one is disobedient it hurts the whole family.

> 1 Cor. 12:25, 26 *...that there should be no division in the body, but that the members should have the same care for one another. And if one member suffers, all the members suffer with it; or if one member is honored, all the members rejoice with it.*

Think about your own family for a moment, if one is disobedi-ent, doesn't it affect everyone? When one of my older children gets in trouble and there is a punishment, my younger children will be the ones crying. It is a natural reaction for them to be disturbed, because we are a family and we love each other and they don't like to see the others punished.

I have seen how the blessing of tithing affects churches that have a congregation that tithes. The people are on fire for Christ, people's lives are radically being changed because of the ministries in the church, and missionaries are being sent out to preach the Gospel.

But mostly, I have seen how tithing and giving has blessed my family and me. So many times, I've been on my knees, crying to God thanking Him for His incredible blessings. I am so unworthy, but by His amazing grace He continues to give back to me so much more than I can comprehend. If only people would realize how much our Father loves us and wants to bless us, if only we will be more obedient and faithful. We think about *good* and God thinks about *best!*

> Ephesians 3:20, 21   *Now to Him who is able to do exceedingly abundantly above all that we ask or think, according to the power that works in us, to Him be glory in the church by Christ Jesus to all generations, forever and ever, Amen.*

Chapter 3 – Tithing
Review Points

- Tithing is a form of worship.

- Tithing is 10% of our gross income of all that comes into the house.

- We are "robbing God" if we do not give back 10% to Him, of which 100% is really His to begin with.

- Tithing is the only topic in the Bible where God challenges us to be obedient so we can see His faithfulness and blessings.

- Abram commenced it, Moses commanded it, Jesus commended it.

Budgeting

Luke 14:28

For which of you, intending to build a tower, does not sit down first and count the cost, whether he has enough to finish it.

Ok, now what? God is the owner and I am His steward. God commands us to give 10% of everything we earn and give it to our home church. God will bless His church and me, and then we will be a tremendous witness to the world. You might be thinking, "That is all well and good, however, I need to learn financial wisdom practically as well as theologically." Fair enough. In this chapter you will learn how to implement a family budget and a net worth statement and most importantly, will learn the purpose of both.

How do we begin? We start with a tool called a budget. We all know this term, but few people actually use a budget. I am going to put in a disclaimer right now and say something that most experts will disagree on. A budget can be written in pencil and not a pen. It is not etched in stone.

A budget is a guide and not an absolute. The process of creating a budget is just as effective as implementing a budget. Income is what you bring in to the household in the form of money. Expenses are what exit your household in the form of bills. A balanced budget is when your income is at least as much as your expenses. We want to create a surplus in our budget. Sounds like our government, doesn't it? Benjamin Franklin said, "There are two ways of making money. Number one is to raise your revenue. Number two is to lower your expenses. But the fastest way is to do both at the same time."

On the next page is *My Personal Budget.* You will need to make a few copies of this. I suggest you put some in a 3 ring binder for future use, and have one taped on a wall by your desk or wherever you pay your bills after it is completed.

I made this particular budget. I like it because it is very descriptive on the items listed and this will hopefully help you to remember every thing that is being purchased. And it is also very easy to use, as you will soon see.

The next step is to write out every purchase you made in the last one to three months. How accurate you want to be will determine how many months you go back. Looking back for one month will only give you a general idea of what you spend money on and will not give you a true picture of your monthly expenses.

It is better to go back three months because some expenses are quarterly, like insurance for example. Repairs and maintenance on homes and cars, gifts, vacations, holidays, subscriptions, and prescriptions are not always monthly. Also, your utility bills fluctuate from month to month. You will get truer numbers going back three months and there won't be as many surprises.

You can do this by going over your checkbook and seeing exactly what you paid for when writing a check. Or, finding your receipts if you use money orders and cash.

Using banks or credit unions and checking accounts is going to be easier if you truly want financial freedom. Believe it or not, almost 40% of the people over 18 years of age use money orders and cash to pay their bills, according to a money order company's research. When I owned check-cashing centers I loved that statistic, but now, it disturbs me.

The main reason people use money orders is that young adults and many people from other countries were never taught how to use

My Personal Budget

Item	Ave/Month 1	Budget/Month 2	Actual/Month 3	Difference/Ave
Giving				
Tithing	$	$	$	$
Charities	$	$	$	$
Food				
Home Consumption	$	$	$	$
Outside the Home	$	$	$	$
Clothing				
Clothing, Shoes	$	$	$	$
Dry Cleaning, Laundry	$	$	$	$
Housing				
Rent or Mortgage	$	$	$	$
2nd Mortgage	$	$	$	$
Real Estate Taxes	$	$	$	$
Home Insurance	$	$	$	$
Furniture, Furnishings	$	$	$	$
Repairs and Maint.	$	$	$	$
Electricity, Gas, Water	$	$	$	$
Telephone, Cable, Net	$	$	$	$
Gardening, House Clean	$	$	$	$
Personal				
Childcare	$	$	$	$
Haircuts, Personal Care	$	$	$	$
Life Insurance	$	$	$	$
Medical				
Medicine	$	$	$	$
Doctor, Dentist, Hospital	$	$	$	$
Health Insurance	$	$	$	$
Automobile				
Car Payments	$	$	$	$
Auto Insurance	$	$	$	$
Gasoline	$	$	$	$
Repairs & Maintenance	$	$	$	$
Miscellaneous				
Vacations	$	$	$	$
Entertainment	$	$	$	$
Education	$	$	$	$
Newspaper, Subscription	$	$	$	$
Other	$	$	$	$
Debt, Savings				
Credit Cards	$	$	$	$
Student Loans	$	$	$	$
Retirement Account	$	$	$	$
Educational Savings	$	$	$	$
Savings Account	$	$	$	$
Total	$	$	$	$

a checkbook or taught to see the benefits. Using money orders can take up so much extra time and it is actually more expensive than writing checks.

When money-order-users get paid, they go to a place to cash their checks and pay a fee for this. Then they will buy money orders for the bills that are due that week and then pay a charge for each money order. The fee for a money order is the same for $10 as it is for $300, and $300 is usually the limit, so any bill over $300 they would have to buy two or more money orders.

It is difficult to get someone with the money order type of system to ever get ahead and think about financial planning. It is more time consuming and expensive and he or she always has cash in their pocket where it is easier to spend also.

Life insurance companies will not let you pay monthly premiums unless it is withdrawn out of your checking accounts. You can pay with a money order on a quarterly, semi-annual, or annual basis, but it is harder to budget for this. In addition, having money automatically transferred from your checking account periodically to an investment is also the easiest and best way to invest. This technique is called *Dollar Cost Averaging.*

Dollar cost averaging is committing a fixed amount at regular intervals to an investment like a mutual fund. The benefit to dollar cost averaging is that you can buy more shares when the price is lower, but you buy fewer shares when the price is up. As you invest over time, your average *cost* per share may be less than the average *price* per share. This way, you can take advantage of the market highs and lows and possibly buy more shares. More shares can mean more dividends. We want as many shares as we can get. We like shares. [See the chart on the next page for an example.]

Now back to our budget. For those people who would like to start fresh and do not want to go browsing through their checkbook nor hunting for all those receipts, there is plan B. Cross out the headings on the My Personal Budget columns from *Average,*

How Dollar Cost Averaging Works

Without				**With**			
Month	Amount Invested	Cost Per Share	Shares Acquired	Month	Amount Invested	Cost Per Share	Shares Acquired
January	$1,000	$10	100	January	$200	$10	20
				February	$200	$8	25
				March	$200	$12.50	16
				April	$200	$8	25
				May	$200	$12.50	16
Total Shares Acquired			100	Total Shares Acquired			102
Average Cost ($1,000/100)			$10	Average Cost ($1,000/102)			$9.80

Dollar cost averaging won't prevent a loss, and it doesn't guarantee investment gains. Investors should consider their financial ability to continue maintaining purchases through periods of low price levels.

Budget, Actual, and *Difference.* Highlight the new headings of *Month 1, Month 2, Month 3,* and *Average.*

Starting in Month 1, write down what you spend on each line item for that first month. (A helpful hint is to keep a running tab on frequent purchases like food and gasoline.) You might have to wait 2 – 4 weeks to continue because of possibly not paying any more bills that month.

Then go to Month 2 and write all the expenses for that second month. And then finally, do the same for Month 3. After the third month, figure out the average dollar amount and put that in the last column.

On a new clean My Personal Budget sheet cross out the headings *Month 1, Month 2, Month 3,* and *Average.* You then put this average number in the first column labeled *Average.* Finally, while you are in your fourth month you will be ready to actually start budgeting.

Obviously this takes much longer. However, you will already experience a commitment to getting your finances in order and you will automatically feel compelled to try to lower your expenses before you begin your actual budget in the fourth month.

You will be amazed at what some of these figures will be. The biggest surprise for most families is food consumed outside the home. Great for the restaurants, coffeehouses, and snack bars, but horrible on your cash flow and waistline.

Entertainment is another sticker shock, especially for Americans. Going to the movies, sporting events and even renting videos adds up very quickly. For many people, *shopping* can be entertainment. We spend entirely too much on fun and do not save nearly enough.

The second column, the *Budget*, is where you put the numbers that are your target figures, the numbers you want to shoot for. Some of these figures will be fixed or the same every month, for example; mortgage or rent, car payments, and childcare if that is necessary. For some others you will want to use the average for the previous three months, for example: utilities, insurance, and gas and oil. The rest of your figures in this second column are the ones you want to try to lower.

There are two very important reasons you want to try to lower the expenses. First, of course, is for the people who do not tithe. This should be a fixed line item. If you are not tithing currently, you may wonder where the money is going to come from. It must come from the areas you are trying to lower or that are "negotiable," such as entertainment and food mentioned a moment ago.

It is personally hard for me to hear people complain about lack of money and then find out they spend $5.00 to $15.00 a day on their lunches and coffee. One gentleman told me how hard he worked every day and that he deserved this "extra" benefit, and that was his only vice. I do not doubt he works hard for the income God has provided for him and his family. However, I know that "brownbagging" it a few days a week would be healthier for him financially, physically, and especially spiritually if he were now able to begin tithing.

The second reason to lower expenses is that we want to be free from consumer debt. If you are in consumer debt, this extra money you find in your budget will go towards eliminating this debt. Getting out of debt will be discussed in the next chapter more thoroughly.

When these first two purposes of lowering expenses are satisfied, tithing regularly and living debt-free, we are then finally able to pursue the next step in The Lord's Financial Plan. This will be explained starting in chapter 6, Financial Planning.

Again, back to our budget. After you have written in your *average* numbers and then figured out your *budget* figures, you then must wait one month. At the end of the fourth month (if you averaged out the previous three months, which I recommend), go back

---

We want to tell our money where to go instead of wondering where it went.

---

and enter what the actual expenses were for this fourth month in the third column labeled *Actual*. Subtract the *actual* dollar amount from the *budget* amount and put the number in the *Difference* column.

This will give you the "difference" of the actual expenditures and the *desired* budgeted amount. This is where some evaluations are going to be made. We are trying to find a surplus. If there is not any extra money at the end of the month, then the "budget" numbers are too lenient.

This is a work in progress and should be adjusted accordingly almost every month. That is why it is so important to understand this is a guide or plan. It should not and can not be a burden. We are trying to find out where the money goes. We want to get to a point where we tell our money where to go, instead of wondering where it all went; that is a budget.

There are a few things that will kill, steal, and destroy your budget. They are called Budget Busters. The first one is impulse items. This is when we buy on the spot for no apparent reasons, other than it looks like a good idea and we want it now. There is a purpose for that merchandise at the check stands, and that is for last-minute impulse purchases. You do not have to think about it long, it's not a major purchase, and it rarely costs very much. But it sure is tempting, isn't it?

When I owned my convenience stores, I had a motto that said, "I only want a quarter more." If I could persuade people to buy one last thing before we checked them out at the register, I would have the increase in dollar per square-foot measurement I was looking for. Next time you are at a major retail chain store, notice all the impulse items by the checkout lines. They have studied buying behaviors of every demographic and they know what it takes for us to buy one more item as we are leaving. Resist the urge to buy at the last moment.

Stereotypically, women will shop for items in a couple of stores and take their time and enjoy themselves. Pastor Charles Stanley of InTouch Ministries calls this activity, "floating through the malls." Where most men on the other hand, will hunt it down and kill it. We go in, find the items, and then leave the store as fast as we can. When using a budget, be a hunter and not a floater.

Another Budget Buster is impatience. You may not see immediate results from using a budget. Many times it takes months to see and feel any financial freedom. It will take discipline and persistence.

Satan will do anything to ruin you. To see you obeying the Lord by your tithing is a direct hit to the devil. You will notice spiritual attacks, but remember, you have the Lord's promise of protection against the enemy. Continue to pray and seek God's wisdom, lay hands on your budget and bills and claim God's promises in His word for your finances. The Bible says *"If God is for me, who can be against me?"*

The last Budget Buster is that the budget is too strict or too loose. If too strict, you will give up because it is too difficult to maintain. Giving up possibly means not tithing and staying in bondage to consumer debt. This will give victory to the enemy.

If it's too loose, then there is no surplus or savings, which could result in no financial plan in the future. This also gives victory to Satan, because without a financial plan we are out of God's will, which we will see in Chapter 6.

A budget is similar to starting a workout program and trying to get in good physical shape. You must exercise, eat healthy, and be disciplined or go back to being out of shape. Using a budget will get you into good financial shape. You will not have to do it forever.

A budget is only needed to create a surplus to tithe, get out of debt, and to start your financial plan. It is a new mentality that must be part of your lifestyle and not be seen as a quick fix. Just like a diet to lose weight. You only do it till you get to your desired weight and then maintain with healthier eating habits.

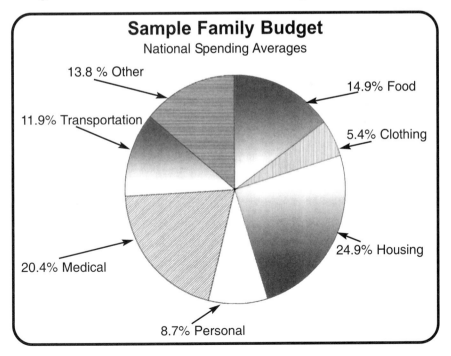

Sample Family Budget
National Spending Averages

- 13.8 % Other
- 14.9% Food
- 11.9% Transportation
- 5.4% Clothing
- 20.4% Medical
- 24.9% Housing
- 8.7% Personal

On the previous page is a sample family budget based on a national average of a husband, wife, and two kids. I've seen these samples in the 70's, 80's, and this one is from 1999, and they are all about the same, give or take a few percentage points. This is more for amusement than a guide – please use it this way.

I would like to share with you a story about a court judge granting a young woman a dollar amount based on these national averages.

I was teaching a small group of abused women, who were getting their lives back together after getting away from their abuser and they wanted some basic fundamentals in getting started financially. After the workshop, a teenage single mom came up to me and asked if she could use the figures and chart the next day for her court hearing on her alimony/child support issue from her ex-husband, because she had no idea how much to ask for from the ex-husband.

I told her to use the numbers because they came from a U.S. Government report. I was told by one of the ministry helpers a month later the wonderful news. The judge sided with the young mother using these national averages as the basis for her child support and she has now been able to start a new life. This story was one of the foundations for this book. Maybe, I thought, more people need to know about the basics of money management, and the earlier they start the better.

It is also very important to know your income on a monthly basis. This might sound like an obvious response, but a lot of people do not know exactly what comes in to the household every month. Invariably, I will ask a couple what their individual income is, and they look at each other with a surprised look because they don't know the answer. Most of the time, they will have to go get a recent paystub to answer my question.

Your income will consist of your salary or wages, interest on savings, dividends from investments, rental income, and child support or alimony if that applies. For those who have a fluctuating income, usually commissioned sales people, just average out your last three or four months and that will suffice for budgeting purposes.

Now you know your revenue and your expenses. As Benjamin Franklin said earlier, attack both at the same time to create a surplus. Here is an idea that you can use today and see the results on your next paycheck. If you raise your exemptions on your W-2 form from the human resource department just one or two more, this will give you a little extra money every pay period. Raising your exemptions to 5 or 6 during November and December will also help with your extra spending during the holidays. Then lower it back down to normal in January.

However, doing this will change your year-end tax situation. Please talk to your tax advisor and/or human resource person at work before doing this. Some people like the idea of getting a tax refund every year. To them it is a forced savings plan. Others are scared to death of having to pay taxes at the end of the year. Personally, I like to have a balance in my tax strategy. I want to use as much as I can during the year without paying taxes at the end of the year. A good accountant should be able to help you with this.

A few more thoughts before we leave this chapter on budgeting. I have always recommended that one person in the family be in charge of keeping the finances up to date. This has nothing to do with traditional roles of marriage, or submission to someone's authority. It simply means whoever is best suited to keep the records straight and current. For example, the checkbook must be balanced every month, the budget reviewed every month, bills paid on time, and the files are to be kept in order. It does not mean this person is Hitler in the household, but someone who best qualifies for the duty.

The person who does the "accounting" also has an added responsibility of making sure the other spouse knows how to take over in case of death or sickness. The "accountant" must show the spouse, or secondary person, how they pay the bills, keep the records, maintain files, and prepare for the tax season. I suggest an annual review with each other to protect against a catastrophe.

What has worked well for me is to make a "year" file, like 2005, for instance. When I prepare for my tax appointment, I will go through each "individual" file and take out the twelve months worth of statements and staple them together. For example, I will gather my bank statements for the year from my bank statement file and staple them or bind them together. Then go to my insurance files and staple them together. Then my investment file. And go through each file in this manner. I then take these to my CPA so they can figure out my taxes for the past year.

Afterward, I will put all of these "bound" papers in the one big file labeled by year, like "2005" as mentioned above. We are supposed to keep our records for seven years. So in this example, I would have shredded all my 1998 paperwork. Now in my individual files, they are empty waiting for the current year stuff. This is an ideal way of preparing for your taxes, keeping your files current, having easy access to statements, and making it easy for someone to take your place if necessary.

For those that are computer literate, there are wonderful financial programs that can make budgeting, check balancing, and year-end tax reporting easier for you. Just make sure your spouse knows how to use it also.

Another helpful hint is to sit down at the bill-paying area at least once a week and pay the bills weekly. This way you will stay current, it won't take as long, and you have better cash management. Sometimes you will sit down with nothing to do. Then you will know that you now have a system in place and you are being the steward God calls you to be.

I also believe there should be one checkbook for the family. If a husband has a checkbook as well as a wife and they are paying different bills, that is a surefire recipe for disaster. If a man and woman are to become one flesh after marriage, then they surely can become one checking account. I know countless Christian couples who will not relinquish control of the finances and there are two checkbooks in the household. This is a pride issue and a trust issue, neither of which is healthy in a marriage.

I have included a Net Worth Statement on the next page. You will have to make copies for your three-ring binder. After you have completed your budget, I recommend you fill out a net worth statement. A net worth statement gives you a starting point to keep score with. Your assets minus your liabilities equal your total net worth.

To do a Net Worth Statement you need to gather all your current statements and transfer the balances to the *Liquid Assets* and the *Investment* sections. The first time you do a net worth statement, use a pencil.

You will have to use your best guess on the *Personal Assets* section. I recommend that you use conservative numbers and not overvalue items that would be hard to liquidate or sell. If you do not know the value of your home, you can call a local real estate agent and ask for some comparable or recent home sales in your area. Make sure you write down what the home is worth and not what you owe on it, because you will list the *Mortgage Loan* amount under *Long Term Liabilities*. If you are a business owner, then you would put what your business is worth, including any inventory, in the *Business* section.

The Liabilities column has three sections, *Short Term, Long Term,* and *Business*. The *Long Term* part can be filled out with the current statements you have previously gathered. The only reasons you would need to fill out the *Short Term* are that you have extremely high utility bills or you pay taxes and insurances quarterly. The *Business* part is for those who have any loans or inventory payments due and then write in the totals where indicated.

You then add up the separate sections. This number will allow you to see where the areas are growing *and* shrinking year after year. Then bring down the totals of the two columns. Subtract the

Net Worth Statement

Liquid Assets

Cash (on hand)	$_____
Checking Account	$_____
Savings Account	$_____
Money Market	$_____
Total	$_____

Personal Assets

Home	$_____
Furniture, Funishings	$_____
Cars, other Vehicles	$_____
Collectibles	$_____
Other Assets	$_____
Total	$_____

Investments

Stocks, Bonds	$_____
Mutual Funds	$_____
IRAs	$_____
Work Retirement Plan:	
vested portion	$_____
Real Estate	$_____
C.D.s	$_____
Life Insurance:	
Cash value	$_____
Other investments	$_____
Total	$_____

Business

Business Value	$_____

Total Assets $_____

Short Term Liabilities

Utilities	$_____
Taxes	$_____
Insurances	$_____
Total	$_____

Long Term Liabilities

Mortgage Loan	$_____
Auto Loans	$_____
School Loans	$_____
Credit Cards	$_____
Other	$_____
Total	$_____

Business

Business Loans	$_____
Inventory	$_____
Total	$_____

Total Liabilities $_____

Net Worth Summary

Total Assets	$_____
Total Liabilities	$_____

(Assets - Liabilities = Net Worth)

Net Worth $_____

Total Liabilities from the Total Assets and this will give you your Net Worth.

A net worth total is a very important amount to know for a couple of reasons. One reason will be discussed later and the other reason is we now have a starting point to begin our financial plan.

At the end of one year, figure out your total net worth again. Do this every year and keep putting them in your 3 ring binder. After each year, see if you are proceeding in the right direction. Ideally you want your net worth to get larger every year. If you are digressing, there is a problem. Your expenses continue to exceed your income, and you are not living within your means. On the other hand, if the trend is going up, you have things under control and you are proving to be a good steward.

Now if something catastrophic occurs, that is another story. An illness, a divorce, a loss of a job, or a death in the family will obviously change the financial picture.

However, cling to God's Word and His promises and you will be victorious. Walking thru the valley is not fun, but the other side is wonderful! I know. I have personally seen the fruits of victory and the agony of defeat.

At times, I needed a CPA to figure out my net worth. At other times I could figure it out myself at a stop sign. I followed the same principles explained in this book. I have almost lost everything and have been in an incredible amount of debt two times, but the Lord was faithful and I tried my best to be obedient. God taught me many things during these devastating trials – lessons I needed to learn.

> Romans 8:28 *And we know that all things work together for good to those who love God, to those who are called according to His purpose.*

Chapter 4 – Budgeting
Review Points

- A budget is a guide and not an absolute.

- The budget is needed to find a surplus.

- This surplus does three things:
    - ✧ Allows us to tithe the correct amount.
    - ✧ Is used to pay off consumer debt.
    - ✧ Creates our funding vehicle to start financial planning.

- We must do a Net Worth Statement to get a starting point.

- Next create a system for bill paying, filing, and tax preparing that can be taught to another person.

Debt Elimination

Romans 13:8a

To owe no one anything except to love one another.

Now is a good time to talk of a notorious four-letter word:

D – E – B – T.

This is a word no one wants to talk about. However, let me say that not all debt is bad because there *is* good debt. Buying a home for your family that has the potential to appreciate in value is not bad debt. Purchasing a practical car for you and your family by using a car loan makes sense. A school loan providing an education to get a well-paying job is debt that is good. Even debt for a business loan from a well-thought-out business plan is a good thing.

What I want to cover in this chapter is the debt caused by consumerism and materialism and the use of credit cards, this is bad debt. I will also explain a plan to get out of this type of "consumer" debt, if this applies to you.

Consumer debt is the liability that causes anxiety in our finances. This kind of debt can become a serious problem when you are not able to pay your regular expenses on time, or if you are getting behind on other financial obligations. This is the debt that gets people in trouble. If worrying about how to pay the credit cards is keeping you up at night, or if you're thinking about taking on a part time job, or having your spouse work more, then you have become a slave to the lender.

> Proverbs 22:7 says, *"The rich rules over the poor, and the borrower is servant of the lender."*

This kind of servitude is not what our Lord had in mind when He tells us to serve one another. Being a slave to the lender causes incredible amounts of worry and anxiety. Heart specialists tell us that the number one source of heart trouble is worry. Physicians say that 70% of all illnesses are imaginary and the reason being worry. We cannot be free from worry and anxiety if we are encumbered with a lot of consumer debt.

> Charles Dickens wrote in *David Copperfield*:
> "Annual income twenty pounds, and annual expenditure nineteen ninety six, results in happiness. Annual income twenty pounds, and annual expenditure twenty pounds ought and six, results in misery."

When Sir Walter Raleigh was burdened with a huge debt, his doctor told him one day if he didn't stop worrying he would die. Sir Walter looked up sadly and said, "I can't help worrying as long as that debt is over my head. It may kill me, but you might as well tell my cook to order the water in the kettle not to boil as to command my brain not to worry."

We must try, with all our might and strength, to let it go and cast all our cares upon the Lord. We are to take our burdens to God and then we must leave them there. Billy Graham once said trust in God is the one answer to anxiety. God has proved over and over that He is trustworthy.

If we are committed to getting out of debt and the bondage it causes, we must bring this burden to God in prayer, and then God will honor this prayer request. We do not have to wonder if this is God's Will or not, because it is being in God's Will to be free from bondage.

Giving our debt problem to God does not alleviate the repercussions of our sin, however. This will not let us off the hook for the

---

It is as much of a sin to covet after a material item as it is to commit adultery; after all, it is the 10ᵗʰ Commandment.

---

problems we have created for ourselves. We are still responsible for our past actions and we must pay for our mistakes. It is as much of a sin to covet after a material item as it is to commit adultery; after all, it is the 10th Commandment. Jesus, Himself, issues a warning about this.

> Luke 12:15 *And He said to them, "Take heed and beware of covetousness, for one's life does not consist in the abundance of the things he possesses."*

A. W. Tozer writes in his book *The Pursuit of God*:

"There is within the human heart a tough, fibrous root of fallen life whose nature is to possess, always to possess. It covets *things* with a deep and fierce passion. The pronouns *my* and *mine* look innocent enough in print, but their constant and universal use is significant. They express the real nature of the old Adamic man better than a thousand volumes of theology could do. They are verbal symptoms of our deep disease. The roots of our hearts have grown down into *things*. And we dare not pull up one rootlet lest we die. Things have become necessary to us, a development never originally intended. God's gifts now take the place of God, and the whole course of nature is upset by the monstrous substitution."

He goes on to say:

"The way to deeper knowledge of God is through the lonely valleys of soul poverty and abnegation of all things. The blessed ones who possess the kingdom are they who have repudiated every external thing and have rooted from their hearts all sense of possessing. These are the "poor in spirit." They have reached an inward state paralleling the outward circumstances of the common beggar in the streets of Jerusalem. That is what the word *poor* as Christ used it actually means. These blessed poor are no longer slaves to the tyranny of things. They have broken the yoke of the oppressor; and this they have done not by fighting but by surrendering. Though free from all sense of possessing, they yet possess all things."

Giving our consumer debt situation to the Lord is the first necessary step in getting out of bondage and getting into the Lord's Financial Plan. Repent and ask for His forgiveness in this area and He will make a way where there seems to be no way of getting out of debt.

Purchasing items because of a *want* and not because it is a *need* will get people in trouble with credit cards. Most people enjoy shopping and buying new things for themselves and others. I admit that I love purchasing stuff for my children, and since I am already out, why not go ahead and buy a lunch or dinner? I'm already spending money and it seems to go hand in hand to buy a meal while shopping.

However, it takes self-control, one of the fruits of the Holy

Spirit, to stay within your budget. A lot of the times, the purchased items are financed; either through the store's credit card or by way of a national credit card like a *VISA* or *MasterCard*. Even if you got a terrific original price, the "good deal" is gone by the time you've finished paying it off – *if* you ever do pay it off.

I have known and still know people who are addicted to shopping. They go to stores every day and purchase items. You might know someone who has this similar problem as well. They *have* to buy something every day. Some will not even open the packages or wear the clothes and then take the product back and get a refund. Then they will turn around and buy something else with this refunded money.

Now imagine the spouse finally catching on and feeling cheated, so what does the spouse do? They spend money equal to what the other one is spending. Now you have a family out of control and in major debt. This is a dark side of addictions that is hardly ever discussed and is one of the factors in divorces caused by financial hardships.

The best way to buy anything is to pay for the whole purchase right then and there with cash, check, or debit card. However, most people cannot wait that long and they put it on a credit card thinking they will pay for it when the statement comes. But if they can't pay for it then, what makes them think they can pay for it in a few weeks?

If people *could* pay off their credit card every month (the proper way to use a credit card), we wouldn't be trillions of dollars in debt. Credit cards in and of themselves are not necessarily bad. In fact, they can be very useful, just like a car can be incredibly helpful. And medicine has its obvious advantages in healing people. But in the wrong hands all of these can be extremely dangerous.

Because people are not able to pay off their credit card amount every month, the interest gets added on and the credit card company gives you this wonderfully low minimum payment amount. The higher the interest rate the lower the minimum payment will be per dollar, because you are paying mostly the interest and the credit card company wants to string you along for as long as possible.

You think you can handle that monthly payment easily enough and you put more and more on it. The minimum payment hardly increases at all and now you have become a victim. People just starting out who are new to credit cards are easily snared by this trap.

> Proverbs 22:16b says   *And he who gives to the rich will surely come to poverty.*

I will say that it might not be a problem with materialism that all items are put on a credit card. It could be those people who have lived on a credit card because of a catastrophe like the loss of a job, a divorce, a long illness, medically necessary expenses, or possibly a death of a loved one. An emergency situation is different than consumerism. When it is a matter of survival then one has to do whatever it takes.

I have been in this position twice before as I mentioned in the last chapter. One time, after a business I started did not work out after about one year and I did not bring in *any* income for several months. I was forced to put necessary expenses on a credit card – actually, on several credit cards.

Another time, I was not earning enough to support my children when I first got started in the financial industry, so I had to put several regular living expenses on a credit card. It was not because I had purchased beautiful Italian designer drapes and soft luscious furniture. It was to buy food, gasoline, and household utilities that went on a credit card.

It is a very humbling experience to be teaching on financial matters and trying to make a living as a new financial planner and not being able to provide for one's own family. I'd reassure myself by saying, "Well, doctors are not always the healthiest people," or "a mechanic's car doesn't always run smoothly," or "professional athletes are not always in the best physical shape."

Credit cards, if used properly by paying the entire balance when due, can work very well. Visa, MasterCard, and American Express are helpful and necessary when making reservations, traveling, and buying on the internet. However, using these cards to purchase tangible or material items *over time* will cost a lot more than you think. This is called the *time value of money*.

Here's how this works: Let's say you want to purchase a new plasma television, DVD, and all the trimmings for a total price of $2500 (notice the word *want*, you do not *need* a new TV). You put it on a credit card which charges you 14% interest. The item starts depreciating (going down in value) by the time it's installed, and the cost of borrowing the money is appreciating (going up) because of the accumulating interest. And a dollar today will always be worth more than a dollar tomorrow because of inflation.

The *cost* is more expensive than the *price* because the values are going the opposite way. The best way to purchase items that depreciate is with cash or with a check. Better yet, buy these types of items used – after they have already had the major depreciation.

I have always bought cars that are at least 2 years old. The car is less expensive, insurance is lower, as well as the licensing and taxes, and it's usually still under the manufacturer's warranty. Next time you want something newer, look for something older. The classified section in newspapers has incredible deals in them. Make them an offer they can't refuse, as Don Corleone says in *The Godfather.*

Department stores, big retail stores, and home improvement stores all offer credit cards. Don't be tempted. You only need one major credit card, either American Express, MasterCard or a Visa. American Express works the best because you have to pay them off at the end of the month. American Express makes most of their money from the annual fee. So get rid of all your credit cards and keep the *one* with the lowest interest rate.

If you do have a problem with consumer debt, here is a *plan* to

Plan to Get Out of Debt

Credit Card	Total Balance	Minimum Payment	Interest Rate	Month 2 Balance	Month 3 Balance	Month 4 Balance	Month 5 Balance	Month 6 Balance	Month 7 Balance
1	$	$	%						
2	$	$	%						
3	$	$	%						
4	$	$	%						
5	$	$	%						

get out of debt. On the facing page is your "Plan to Get Out of Debt" worksheet. The first column is to list all the credit cards and finance companies, including your mortgage if you have one. The second column is to list the total balances owed to pay off the debt. The third is for the infamous minimum payment.

Remember, the credit card company is going to keep this as low as legally possible. And why not? They are going to make a fortune off this balance. Very little comes off the principle and the rest of the payment is towards the interest.

I wish I had a gazillion dollars and I would have my own Joseph's Visa. As good as I think I am as an advisor, I cannot invest and get a guaranteed annual return of 14% or more, and the credit card makes this interest on millions of dollars every year. The credit card company also charges an annual fee and late charges; is it any wonder they are so profitable? And finally, the last column in the worksheet is for the interest rate percentage.

Remember that this is a *plan* to get out of debt. You must *want* to get out of debt and to be in God's will. You must want to be free and not a slave.

Christians cannot be held in bondage to debt any longer. If you have been irresponsible in the past regarding money and misuse of credit and debt, repent now and ask for forgiveness. You must turn away from the past mistakes of materialism and ask God for the victory in your finances. Ask God for wisdom and strength and He will bless you!

> Psalm 118:5, 6 *I called on the Lord in distress; the Lord answered me and set me in a broad place. The Lord is on my side; I will not fear. What can man do to me?*

The very first thing you can do to help yourself immediately is to call your credit card companies today. Tell them you are being inundated with other credit card offers and you would like to stay where you are; however, you need a lower interest rate. They will honor this request if you have a good payment history with them. You will be pleasantly surprised how low your new rate will be.

I was helping a seminary professor once with his budgeting and debt problems and told him to go home and call his credit card companies. He e-mailed me back the same day and told me the rate went from 16.9% to 2.9% on one card and the other card went from 12.9% to 7.9%. All it took was asking.

Now then, you need to go back to your personal budget and find out how much is going towards your debt obligations. Pay the minimum payments – yes, this is correct – pay the minimum towards all the debts *except* the one with the highest interest rate. This high interest rate is the one hurting the most. Pay as much as you can, by using your personal budget, toward this one debt. When that one is paid in full, put a line through it and attack the next highest interest rate debt, still using the same total dollar amount as before.

Pay the minimums on all other credit cards and now attack the next highest interest rate card. Do this until it is paid in full and put a line through it, and so on and so on until everybody and everything is paid off. Please understand, you are doing this with the commitment of not putting anything new on the credit cards!

That is the plan I like best, attacking the highest interest rate, because of the time value of money. I've seen other plans that say to pay off the lowest balance first. Yes, that will work; it's just not as effective. Now if you have a low balance on a credit card and it is within a couple of percentage points of the highest card, go ahead and get rid of that smaller payment. It does give you a psychological feeling of accomplishment and victory. The most important truth is to get out of debt – use either plan, and just learn to be free!

The Israelites, after they were freed from Egypt's bondage, did not know how to live properly in God's Will. They rejoiced for a while and then went back to their previous behavior. They wanted to go back to their old lifestyle. Even after seeing God's miracles to free them after 400 years of slavery, and after praying to be free for 400 years, they felt the need to go to where they were comfortable, in bondage.

Once you are free from debt, you must continue to ask God for wisdom to stay out of debt. The devil will not let up. He will try to entice and tempt you into buying with credit with lies such as, "You got out of debt and trouble once, you can do it again," or "You deserve it for all the sacrifices you made." Don't fall for it.

When I teach a class or give a talk about consumer debt, people will without fail ask me this one question, "I have so much debt I'll never get out of it. Should I declare bankruptcy?" They *never* like my answer of "no." First of all, it is scriptural to pay your obligations.

> Jesus said to His disciples in Mathew 5:37 *Let your "yes" be "yes" and your "no" be "no."*

When we sign an agreement to pay the payments that are on a credit card bill we have made an oath with that company to pay on time or pay additional fees. We need to keep our word and our witness and pay the amount on the statement.

Secondly, declaring bankruptcy only fixes the symptom and does not address the problem. If the bankruptcy courts made it harder for people to declare bankruptcy and made them work the problem out, there would not be nearly the problem of consumer debt we have today. It is much easier to go bankrupt than it is to plan, budget, and sacrifice to get out of debt. Consumer bankruptcy hurts the stores, which in turn have to raise the prices for their losses and then *everyone* pays for the mistakes of a few.

In the olden days you would be put into debtor's prison for not paying your bills and then, not being able to work to pay down your debt, you would stay in prison. This would make you really think about whether to get a loan or not. People who have had a lot of debt very seldom get back into debt problems, if they get out of debt by working a plan. They know how blessed it is to be free and they don't want to go back, ever!

Lastly, going bankrupt will destroy your credit report for up to ten years, but from what I understand you can get your bankruptcy off your credit rating after only two years now; it is just a matter of how much money you want to pay. This does not help the problem at all.

If you go to a bankruptcy lawyer, he will recommend that you declare bankruptcy. The more people that get in trouble with credit card debt, the more need for bankruptcy attorneys, and the result is more bankruptcies. Going bankrupt perpetuates the misconception that you are not responsible for your actions and do not have to pay the price for them. The true consequence of bankruptcy is higher prices for everyone.

The first time I was in financial trouble after some business deals, I went to an attorney for advice. He immediately told me to declare bankruptcy. I was shocked. I was looking for options, not a quick fix that would hurt me for years. He told me, "If I was a doctor and you needed surgery and I performed the surgery and saved your life, would you be upset with me because there was a scar?" He was persuasive, but I held to my convictions, and by God's amazing grace, I got out of the trouble. It took a couple of years to pay everyone, but I did it and kept my word, my witness, and my good credit score.

While we are on the subject of credit scores, it is your *responsibility* to know what your credit report looks like. If you are married, you need to get your spouse's report, also. It is extremely easy to get your credit report and it is now free! Go to the website, *www.annualcreditreport.com* or call 877-322-8228 to get your credit reports from the three major credit bureau agencies – Equifax, TransUnion, and Experian. You will be able to print it out right then and there. Your credit score is not included on the free report, but you can request it for a fee of about $7.00.

This should be done at the very minimum of every two years.

You will be surprised at what you will find on your credit report if you haven't checked it in a long time. Most people have never seen their report, but other companies, lenders, and agencies have seen yours. That is how they determine what type of credit risk we are and what types of offers are available to people with similar payment histories.

Our credit report tells credit agencies how good or bad we are in paying on time. It says how much we owe everyone. It also tells how much we have available to us to get into even more debt, our credit limit. This is our debt ratio, in other words, our ability to borrow. All this information is tabulated into a three digit number, which is our FICO (the Fair Isaac Corp.) score. The higher the number, the better, and the highest is 850. Anything over 650 is good and over 700 is even better.

The formula for our FICO scores works like this: We start with

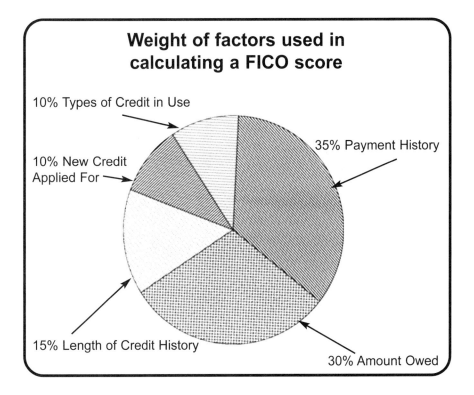

Weight of factors used in calculating a FICO score

10% Types of Credit in Use

10% New Credit Applied For

35% Payment History

15% Length of Credit History

30% Amount Owed

a neutral score of 600 and it goes up or down based on our activity. There are five factors that affect this number. 35% is based on how we have paid our credit obligations in the past. Points are added if we pay on time or subtracted if we pay late. The more credit we have used and paid on time, the better our score. 30% is based on our debt-to-available-credit ratio. The lower that ratio, the higher our score would be. 15% is based on the amount of time we have managed credit. The longer our credit history is, the better our score will be. 10% is based on how many different types of credit we have had. The last 10% of our score is based on how many new credit applications we have initiated ourselves. The pre-approved applications that come in the mail do not hurt the score, unless we actually take them up on the new offer.

Why do I mention the credit report? First of all, as I mentioned, it is your responsibility. Part of being a good steward. Secondly, if you have been faithful to God's Will in your finances, He may decide to bless you with a nicer home in a neighborhood with better schools, or possibly a newer car, or maybe even a business of your own.

The first place a lender looks is your credit report. It is wise to start fixing any errors and getting your FICO score higher as soon as you can. It can also help protect you and your family from identity theft by staying on top of it.

All the credit report bureaus will tell you how to correct any mistakes when they send your report. And believe me, if you have not done it for a long time, there will be errors. Watch for misspelled names, wrong addresses, and incorrect employers, because it could possibly mean that someone has opened an account in your name. These types of mistakes can be corrected by contacting the credit reporting agency directly by phone or online. For the more serious mistakes, you will want to have a paper trail, so write to the bureau by certified mail and request a return receipt.

Credit Reporting Agencies

Equifax, P.O. Box 740241, Atlanta, GA. 30374-0241
800-685-1111
Experian, P.O. Box 2104, Allen, TX. 75013-2104
888-397-3742
Trans Union, P.O. Box 2000, Chester, PA. 19022
800-888-4213

I must admit that there is one debt that can never be paid in full. That is our sin debt. If this debt does not get paid in full, then there is a penalty far greater than late fees and high interest. Its penalty is separation from God forever and spending eternity in Hell.

By God's awesome grace and love, His son Jesus came to pay this sin debt in full. His payment took all the past, present, and future sins of all of mankind and stamped it, "Paid in full!" He paid for this debt with His life, in the most agonizing way by being crucified on a cross. The only thing we have to do is receive this wonderful free gift of salvation and all our sins will be gone. There are only three simple steps to take and it can be done right now.

* Admit your condition before God. *"I am a sinner who needs forgiveness."*

* Recognize Jesus Christ as God's only solution to our condition. *"I believe that Jesus died for all my sins."*

* Receive Jesus Christ as your Savior and Lord. *"I now invite you to come into my heart and life. I trust you as my Savior and I will follow you as my Lord."*

We are here on this earth to make a decision and we *will* spend eternity with the consequence of that decision. We are either living with God or living with Satan. Jesus says we are either for Him or against Him. There is nothing we can do to earn this free gift of salvation except to receive it tangibly. Make that commitment now to receive Jesus Christ as your Savior and Lord and put your trust in Him.

> 1 John 5:11-13 *And this is the testimony: that God has given us eternal life, and this life is in His Son. He who has the Son has life; he who does not have the Son of God does not have life. These things I have written to you who believe in the name of the Son of God, that you may know that you have eternal life, and that you may continue to believe in the name of the Son of God.*

Chapter 5 – Debt Elimination Review Points

- Consumer debt is usually the problem that creates anxiety in our finances.

- Use a plan to get out of debt – ASAP!

- Use your budget alongside your debt plan.

- Our credit report is our responsibility and needs to be reviewed at least every other year.

- Our "sin debt" can only be paid by one person – Jesus Christ, the Son of God.

Financial  Planning

Proverbs 13:12

Hope deferred makes the heart sick, but when the desire comes, it is a tree of life.

This is the second half of the book, which will explain what financial planning is in a practical way. It will discuss the tools available to you, and the sequence of steps to create your financial plan. We will see what our Lord says about financial planning and the Biblical aspect to planning for the future.

Actually, the first half is the most significant, because it is critical to understand our role and motives as stewards and to comprehend the idea of being free from financial bondage. Afterward, we are free to hope, free to plan, free to invest, and free to give.

Since we are stewards of everything God has given us, I believe we should be proactive in our stewardship. We must start to plan for our finances, plan for our future and if the Lord wills, plan for our fortune. God Himself is the Master Planner. He planned every single thing from the beginning; the creation of the universe, Heaven and earth, night and day, land and water, animal and man. The Lord planned marriage and procreation, ecology and reproduction, salvation and the redemption of our sins.

I teach a kindergarten class at my church, Pomona First Baptist in California. These children are my "little lambs" and I absolutely love being with them every week. One Sunday morning, they helped me to understand how much planning God did from the very beginning.

I was explaining about the Creation in the book of Genesis, and going over each day of the Creation and what God made on each day. I kept asking, "What do you think God created next?" and they answered, "He made the animals!" "No, not yet" was my reply and I would explain what God created that particular day. "What do you think God did next?" and they would say, "He made the animals!" "No, not yet," I said laughing.

I explained that the animals could not live on the earth until there was land to walk on. The animals couldn't survive on earth without fresh water to drink. The animals could not be made until there were grass and fruit to eat for their food.

As basic as this might sound, it really showed me how much planning God did from the very beginning. I suggest you read Psalm 104 for a beautiful rendition of the Creation and how instrumental every aspect of God's Plan was from the origin of time.

Another classic example of how God plans is the story of Noah and the ark. We usually see a cute picture of a relatively small boat with a house in the middle and animals walking around on a deck, but this is nothing like the real thing. The Hebrew word for "ark" does not mean boat. It means "box". Remember the Ark of the Covenant? It was a box designed to carry the Ten Commandments in. Noah's Ark was designed to carry all the animals and the future of the human race in an enormous box.

Noah built the ark exactly to God's plans and it was perfectly calculated by God to handle the rough seas. The ark was six times longer than it was wide. Modern ocean vessels like aircraft carriers and oil tankers are still built using this same ratio.

When it was fully loaded, the ark displaced about 22 feet of water. Since the ark was 45 feet high, just about half of the ark was submerged, with the other half above the water line. That is the perfect ratio for stability in the water. Even in the biggest waves, the ark could be tilted to almost 90 degrees and still be able to right itself.

Inside, the ark would be able to hold the same amount of cargo as 522 railroad cars could, according to Tom Dooley who wrote *The True Story of Noah's Ark*.   God knew exactly how much space would be needed for all the food, water, animals, roaming room, and flying room.   God had a perfect plan and design for Noah's Ark.

God had a plan for Moses and the two to three million Israelites, plus all their animals, after leaving Egypt.   According to the Quartermaster General in the Army, they would have to have 1500 tons of food every day and 11 million gallons of water every day to drink, cook, and clean with.   They would have used 4000 tons of firewood a day to cook with and to keep warm.   Just think, they did this for forty years!   Moses could not have planned this on his own wisdom.   It was God's supernatural plan that kept the Israelites alive in the desert.

We who have surrendered our lives to Jesus Christ and have the right to be called the children of God, have heard from the beginning of our new life in Christ, that God designs a specific plan utilizing our unique gifts and talents for His kingdom.   God has made a plan for our lives and we can know this because it says so in His Word.

> Jer. 29:11   *"For I know the plans I have for you,"*
> *declares the Lord, "plans to prosper you and not to*
> *harm you, plans to give you hope and a future."*

If God is a planner and we are to be like Him, then it makes sense that we are to plan, as well.   Jesus talks about planning for the future in a parable, the Parable of the Unjust Steward in Luke chapter 16 beginning at verse 1:

> *He also said to His disciples: "There was a certain*
> *rich man who had a steward, and an accusation was*
> *brought to him that this man was wasting his goods.*
> *So he called him and said to him, 'What is this I*

hear about you? Give an account of your steward-ship, for you can no longer be steward.' Then the steward said within himself, 'What shall I do? For my master is taking the stewardship away from me. I cannot dig: I am ashamed to beg. I have resolved what to do, that when I am put out of the steward-ship, that they may receive me in their houses.'

Verse 5 "So he called every one of his master's debtors to him, and said to the first, 'How much do you owe my master?' And he said, 'A hundred measures of oil,' So he said to him, 'Take your bill, and sit down quickly and write fifty.' Then he said to another, 'And how much do you owe?' So he said, 'A hundred measures of wheat.' And he said to him, 'Take your bill, and write eighty.' So the master commended the unjust steward because he had dealt shrewdly. For the sons of this world are more shrewd in their generation than the sons of light."

I must admit I did not understand this parable for a long time. Why would Jesus commend the steward and his dishonesty? Especially after first wasting the master's goods and then after-wards cheating his master by lowering the bills to others.

But, Jesus is not praising the unjust steward for acting deceit-fully, but for thinking ahead and planning for his future, a future without a job. There are a few theories on the reduction of repay-ment, such as reducing the excessive interest the unjust steward previously charged, or taking off all interest altogether. Another theory and what I believe is, the steward subtracted his own com-mission to the debtors, which would lower the bill and not hurt the master.

This way the steward has sacrificed what he could have taken now and has given it to others so that he can receive gain later. In this way he is seen as generous and worthy of praise.

Since the steward was doing great favors for these people, they in turn would be obligated to him and possibly let the steward stay at their home or maybe give him a job. People in that area at that time of history, and still to this day, are extremely hospitable. If the steward had nowhere else to go, the people he gave favors to would take care of him by housing him and feeding him.

He was planning for his future and that is more than most Christians do. Reread the last part of Luke 16:8.

> *So the master commended the unjust steward because he had dealt shrewdly. For the sons of this world are more shrewd in their generation than the sons of light.*

In the Greek language, the word *shrewd* means to act with fore-sight. In English, the definition is: acute in perception and sound in judgment. *Shrewdly* is the key word or lesson that Jesus wants us to learn in this parable. To think ahead, plan for the unknown, and to count the costs.

A similar lesson is in the Parable of the Wise and Foolish Virgins in Mathew 25: 1-4, as Jesus is teaching His disciples.

> *Then the kingdom of Heaven shall be likened to ten virgins who took their lamps and went out to meet the bridegroom. Now five of them were wise and five were foolish. Those who were foolish took their lamps and took no oil with them, but the wise took oil in their vessels with their lamps.*

The foolish five were unprepared for anything else other than a perfect situation, and the wise five realized there could be a detour, delay, or dead-end and were ready for the future by bringing extra oil with them.

I have a theory on why Christians as a whole do not plan for their future. I believe there are two reasons. The first is, if you have studied the Bible, you will realize that about 25% of God's Word talks about prophesy, and the "end times" and the Second Coming of Christ. One of the prophesies is the promise of Jesus Himself coming in the clouds and taking all the Christians back to Heaven with Him.

> 1 Thes. 4:17 *Then we who are alive and remain shall be caught up together with them in the clouds to meet the Lord in the air. And thus we shall always be with the Lord.*

Since we know Jesus could come back at any second, Believers do not spend enough time planning ahead in case Jesus does not come back in our lifetime. Looking at our world today, it looks a lot like what the Bible talks about during the "end times." But we have no idea when Jesus is coming back – no one does – even Jesus says it is only the Father who knows. It could be in 5 minutes, 5 years, or 500 years from now. So we must be prepared whether Jesus comes back today or in 100 years. Jesus says in Mathew 24: 45, 46,

> *"Who then is a faithful and wise servant, whom his master made ruler over his household, to give them food in due season? Blessed is that servant whom his master, when he comes, will find so doing."*

The Lord wants His servants to plan for the future and calls us blessed for doing so. It is our responsibility and part of our role as a good steward.

The second reason I believe Christians do not plan is because we have heard several times that we are to be content in all things, and the love of money is the root of all evil. Since financial planning revolves around money, we fear we might be sinning in this area, that we might accidentally get consumed with money. And we do not want God to take away our current financial blessings from us. So Christians live day to day and week to week and let God take care of them with no planning on their part. But by not planning ahead, Christians lose out on even greater blessings from God.

Paul tells us in Philippians 4:11-12 that whatever state we are in, rich or poor, hungry or full, to be with or without, that we should be content. This is, of course, very true. The very nature of God is love and He will always take care of His children. Verse 19 of this same chapter in Philippians says,

> *And my God shall supply all your needs according*
> *to His riches in glory by Jesus Christ.*

Even though we are to be content in all things, there is nothing in the Scriptures that says planning and accumulating possessions is sinful. However, I will point out, there are many *dangers* involved in acquiring wealth. There are more temptations connected with the pursuit of wealth, which can lead to destruction. It is the *desire* to be rich for the sake of being rich, rather than to be *content* with our riches.

I read one time where an author said that those who have been blessed by God with material wealth should never despise the blessing but rather should heed the warnings. Paul writing to his protégé, Timothy, confirmed this.

> 1 Timothy 6:6-10 *Now godliness with contentment*
> *is great gain. For we brought nothing into this*
> *world, and it is certain we can carry nothing out.*
> *And having food and clothing, with these we shall be*
> *content. But those who desire to be rich fall into*
> *temptation and a snare, and into many foolish and*
> *harmful lusts which drown men in destruction and*

> *perdition. For the love of money is a root of all kinds of evil, for which some have strayed from their faith in their greediness, and pierced themselves through many sorrows.*

I read this *very* morning in *Our Daily Bread,* an excellent daily devotional, and it could not have been a coincidence, a poem written by Dennis De Haan that said:

> If money is your highest goal,
> The thing you long to gain,
> Its power will enslave your soul
> And cause your life much pain.

When we read and hear sermons about the *love* of money being the root of all evil, we mistakenly hear it saying to us that *money* is the root of all evil. Many Christians have read this incorrectly when it comes to planning for the future. We may lose some of our drive or our ambition for success. We then question our motives.

Decide if your financial plan is a personal desire for money or if it is obedience to God's Word.

God is not the author of confusion. God wants us to be prosperous and successful because that glorifies Him, and it is a reflection of His goodness and provision to His children. What we need to do is decide if our financial planning is a personal desire for money out of pride or if it is obedience to God's Word. We should pray and meditate on scripture to help us decide where our motives are coming from.

I know this self-evaluation happened to me. I was modestly successful in my field of business when I got saved. I remember reading in the Book of James and I was so convicted in my efforts to become rich. I relied on and trusted in *my* equity in my business-es. James is straightforward and will shoot you between the eyes at times. These are the verses that weighed heavy on my heart.

> James 1:9-11 *Let the lowly brother glory in his exal-tation, but the rich in his humiliation, because as a flower in the field he will pass away. For no soon-er has the sun risen with a burning heat than it with-ers the grass; its flowers fall, and its beautiful appearance perishes. So the rich man also will fade away in his pursuits.*

After this, I felt guilty and ashamed for striving so hard toward financial success. However, I can justify almost anything, and I thought about how much I was able to give and provide for. But in reality, the fact was, *I* liked the idea of *me* having a lot of money to spend the way *I* wanted to.

I then started selling most of my businesses and ended up where I started, with a partnership in one small market. My focus changed, and it needed to, because I was *too* driven and I was accu-mulating out of pride.

However, I over-corrected, because a portion of my income went with each business I sold. I struggled financially for many years after this paradigm shift. I think I now have the proper bal-ance. Yes, I believe God will always take care of me, and yes, I still need to plan for the future and take care of my family financially.

I believe those are the two *spiritual* reasons why people don't plan financially. One is that Jesus is coming back at any moment and why should they waste their time, money, and energy. The other is having a fear of allowing money to be too much of a prior-ity in their lives and then money becoming a god in their lives.

The *practical* reason is many people think they do not have enough assets to do a financial plan and/or they cannot afford it. That is a myth. Almost every adult needs a plan and most advisors are willing to help at no cost. If the advisor believes a product should be purchased by the client to help in the financial plan, they will make a commission or a fee on that sale. That is how we make our living, either commissions, fees, or both. On the other hand, if you have a large net worth, then a more sophisticated financial plan is probably necessary, and then you might have to pay a planner for this service.

There are many aspects to financial planning. Because of this, people are intimidated by it. That is why I try to keep it extremely simple. I have broken it down into three main categories:

a) Protection
b) Accumulation
c) Preservation

Financial planning doesn't necessarily have a specific order or sequence of events, because you can do different parts simultaneously. For example, you could be accumulating wealth by contributing in your company's retirement plan and be setting up a trust and will for the preservation of your "estate." Or, you might be protecting your family with life insurance in case of a premature death, and buying a house, which is adding to the accumulation of assets. However, I want to caution the people that spend so much time and effort in accumulating assets that they do not see the importance of the other two categories of financial planning and neglect them.

Would it help your spouse and children to be maximizing your contributions in retirement plans and then suddenly die without a life insurance plan to protect your family? No. Would it benefit your family and your favorite non-profit organizations if you had accumulated a large amount and then were to die without an estate plan (preservation) in place? No. Can you see why the accumulation part must be done *with* the other two aspects of financial planning in mind?

We will go through the three main categories of financial planning individually in the remaining chapters. It is my hope and prayer that this book becomes a reference for you – a place to go for answers. The Lord wants us to know and understand money; in fact, He wants us to make friends with it. Let's go back to the end of Jesus' Parable of the Unjust Steward, Luke 16 starting at verse 9:

> *"And I say to you, make friends for yourselves by unrighteous mammon, that when you fail, they may receive you into an everlasting home. He who is faithful in what is least is faithful in much; and he who is unjust in what is least is unjust also in much. Therefore if you have not been faithful in the unrighteous mammon, who will commit to your trust the true riches? And if you have not been faithful in what is another man's, who will give you what is your own? No servant can serve two masters: for either he will hate the one and love the other, or else he will be loyal to one and despise the other. You cannot serve God and mammon."*

Mammon is Aramaic for wealth and Jesus calls it unrighteous. Mammon is called unrighteous not because it is inherently evil but because of the unrighteous attitudes the pursuit of money can produce. Money is the least of all things; however, it can be used to glorify God.

Jesus tells us to learn about and understand money and make friends with it. Learn how to make it work for you, its concepts, its principles, because if we are faithful with the least of all things (money), then we will be faithful with much and what is most important. And that is the true riches the Lord speaks of at the end of verse 11.

I believe the true riches are the gifts of the Holy Spirit; love, joy, peace, patience, kindness, goodness, faithfulness, gentleness, and self-control. For we cannot serve two masters. We *serve* God and *use* money. Money can be a tremendous servant but an absolutely terrible master. The way we handle wealth is a preparatory lesson for our other responsibilities before God.

As we enter the second half of the Lord's Financial Plan, I am reminded of what Jesus tells His twelve disciples.

> Mathew 10:16 *"Behold, I am sending you out as sheep among the wolves. Therefore, be wise as serpents and harmless as doves."*

Chapter 6 – Financial Planning Review Points

- God is the Master-Planner and we are to be like Him, so we must plan as well.

- Financial planning is part of our role as a good steward.

- The three major sections of financial planning are:
  - ✦ Protection
  - ✦ Accumulation
  - ✦ Preservation

- Jesus says to make friends with money and to understand financial principles.

Protection

1 Timothy 5:8

But if anyone does not provide for his own, and especially for those of his household, he has denied the faith and is worse than an unbeliever.

The first category to look at in financial planning is protection. The protection part is probably the most overlooked, because a lot of people do not realize what needs to be protected and for what reason.

One of the things we are protecting is our financial future when there is a death in the family of one of the wage earner's or the caretaker. We also need to protect our tangible assets the Lord has entrusted to us such as homes, cars, and personal belongings from unforeseen accidents. We need to protect our future earnings from a disability and possible liability lawsuits. Finally, we need protection from unplanned emergencies. I will explain each of these in detail and you will have an understanding why protection is always the place to start.

The first thing I am going to talk about is something nobody wants to talk about, and that is life insurance. Life insurance, in its simplest terms, replaces the income of a wage earner when that person dies. As I stated in the last chapter, it does not make sense to *start concentrating solely* on accumulating assets. A premature death would leave the family in a financial nightmare, because now there is no income stream.

I am sure you know of people this has happened to. Think of

the September 11, 2001 tragedies. I read many stories of very successful people who were killed that day and they did not have any additional life insurance other than their work group policy. These families, among many other horrific ordeals, were forced to move out of their homes. Many young adults think that an early death will not happen to them and their families are unprepared if it does.

How many years will your investments last in providing for your family if you die as a young adult? A proper life insurance plan will replace the income of the wage earners for decades and not leave the family destitute in case of a premature death.

However, not *everyone* needs a life insurance policy, but if they do, the amount of life insurance needed goes up and down throughout that person's life. Only a person who has dependants or others depending on his or her income, needs to have life insurance. For example, a child does not need a life insurance policy, because no one is dependent on the child's income.

Some life insurance salesmen are gritting their teeth over that last sentence. They will claim the parents need a policy for the

---

Life insurance replaces the income of a wage earner when that person dies.

---

child's funeral in case the child dies prematurely. An individual policy on a child is unnecessary. If you have done everything I recommend by the end of this book and there is still plenty of money left over, then and only then does it make sense to purchase a "permanent" type of life insurance policy for a child. I'll explain the different types of life insurance shortly.

If you are a single adult and do not have any people dependent on you, such as children or parents, then you do not have a need for life insurance. For the people who do need this important tool of protection, the amount of life insurance needed changes in their lifetime, as you can see in the following graph.

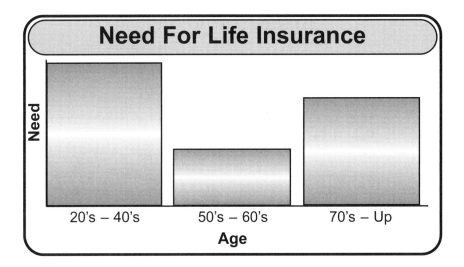

The need is greatest for a young family starting out. Typically, the wife and children will be very dependent on Dad making a living to support them. If he should die prematurely, how would this family survive financially without his income?

The death benefit of life insurance should take care of all the immediate money needs, like funeral expenses, debt, some monthly expenses for time off to regroup, and also most or all the future needs for this family, such as the mortgage or rent and the education of the children.

After the death, the widow might want to go back to school for a higher degree or training so she could get a better job with medical benefits and a good retirement package. All this is taken care of by a well-thought-out life insurance plan.

On the other side of the coin, what if the stay-at-home parent and caretaker should die at a young age? How would the father take care of his children? How would he provide for his family without the help of daycare, babysitters, or a nanny and without the payout of a life insurance policy?

Life insurance cannot replace Mom and Dad, but it can allow the continuation of the same lifestyle. The grieving family has been through enough already. They will receive a check from the life insurance company four or five weeks later and realize their financial future is not in jeopardy. A good sound life insurance plan will provide for their children's children.

>   Proverbs 13:22 *"A good man leaves an inheritance to his children's children."*

When the family gets older, the children eventually move out to start their own lives (hopefully), the mortgage is almost paid off (hopefully), and it costs less to provide for the household (again, hopefully). Add the fact that people usually earn more money when they are in their 50's and 60's. This in turn means they can put more into a retirement account and invest in other areas. During this period, the amount of life insurance needed goes down, because there is less dependence on the income of the wage earner. This doesn't necessarily mean the need goes away. It just means the *amount* of life insurance can be lowered.

If a family has been obedient and has not experienced too many catastrophes in their lives, there might be an estate to protect. Life insurance is the best instrument for the problem of estate taxes, *if* you are still insurable. We will discuss this in detail in the preservation section of the book. So as the graph on the previous page shows, the amount of life insurance needed shoots up again when you get older.

There are several uses for life insurance in the business world. Key man insurance, buy-sell agreements, deferred compensation plans, and executive bonus plans are examples, however, that will not be discussed in this book. But I sure wish I had known about a couple of these when I was a small-business owner.

Life insurance comes in many varieties and has evolved into better products just like any other industry. Life insurance is available in two broad categories:

1.) Term – is very inexpensive and is set for a specific period of time.
2.) Permanent – is in force until the death of the insured and it is expensive.

Term insurance can be a term of employment or a 10 year, 15 year, 20 or 30 year term policy. At the end of that specific term there will be no more insurance for that individual. Ninety-eight percent of all term policies ever written since 1900 have lapsed without the insurance company having to pay a death claim, according to a study done by a university a few years ago.

That is why it is so inexpensive. The insurance company knows they are going to pay out only 2% of the time. This fact does not devalue the need; it is just the way it is. For a family just starting out, there is not a better way to protect the family in case of a premature death than an inexpensive term policy.

I should go back to what I said about a parent not needing an *individual* policy on the child's life. A new family with small children can add a child "rider"; a rider is a benefit that would be attached to a policy of one of the parents for a nominal fee. This is usually a death benefit for $5,000 to $10,000 each on *all* the children if any child should die before the age of eighteen. The cost is very minimal and it would take care of the funeral expenses if this horrendous tragedy occurred.

The problem of term insurance is that it runs out and there is no life insurance in place after the term ends. However, most of today's term policies have an automatic trigger in place at the end of the term and it will continue until death. The main hindrance to this, though, is that the monthly premiums skyrocket as if you were just starting brand new at this advanced age.

Term policies have the same premium amount for the life of the term policy. For example, it might cost $185 a year for a healthy 25-year-old male for a $500,000 ten-year term policy. The payments would remain the same annual amount of $185 for ten years. At the eleventh year, however, the annual payment will go up, because the insurance company now reconfigures the payment on a healthy 36 year-old male. The new annual price for a $500,000 term policy is $1685, almost ten times higher. The next year the insurance company will do this again and have a new price that will go up again because that person is now 37 years old, and so on and on it goes every year.

Term Life Insurance Premiums
10 year term $500,000 policy
for a healty 25-year-old male

Clients Age	Year	Annual Premiums
25	1	$185
(Premium remains constant for first ten years)		
34	10	$185
(significant increase starting year 11)		
35	11	$1,685
(Premium increases annually thereafter)		
39	15	$2,065
40	16	$2,185
44	20	$3,035
45	21	$3,340
49	25	$4,590
50	26	$4,935
54	30	$6,990

The positive aspect to the above scenario is that you do not have to go through "underwriting" ever again. This is the process of determining your insurability by the insurance company's underwriters. If you were to contract a fatal disease, have major heart problems, or even start a dangerous hobby or vocation, you would still be insured. But if you tried to get another life insurance policy, the insurance company would go through the underwriting process over again and declare you are too much of a risk and you might not be able to get insurance.

We, the insured, only think about the monthly premium amount, and the underwriters always think, "How soon do we have to pay the whole amount of the death benefit?"

In essence, the above example of a term policy would basically become a permanent policy because you could not get new insurance and you would have to continue paying the newer and higher rates every year till your death. Or worse yet, the policy lapses or ends because you could not afford to pay any longer because the premiums just got too expensive. Now you are uninsured *and* uninsurable.

You might be wondering how long the term policy should be when applying for the life insurance. Have the term policy for the primary wage earner go until the youngest child turns twenty-two. By then you will have protected your family until the littlest one has graduated from college. For life insurance on the non-working spouse, you only need to go until the youngest child turns fourteen or fifteen. Try telling a 16 year old they need a baby sitter and someone will be filling out your death claim that evening.

The other type of life insurance is called a permanent policy. It is permanent and does not have a fixed period of time like a term policy. The insurance company knows you will die eventually and they *must* pay the death benefit, therefore this type of life insurance is much more costly. There are many kinds of permanent life insurance policies. Senior citizens might remember one being called a whole life policy, because it went your whole life.

Some of the newer permanent policies have an investment added to the death benefit amount. These have a "separate account" with a portfolio of mutual funds in them and hopefully this separate account goes up in value. This separate account investment total is then added to your life insurance policy's death benefit amount when you die.

For example, let's say the death benefit was $300,000 and the separate account had grown to $25,000 the total amount to the beneficiaries would be $325,000. This type of insurance is called a Variable Universal Life or VUL. It is called variable because the mutual funds in the separate account vary from day to day, like any other mutual fund investment, and then the *total* death benefit would also vary from day to day.

The mutual funds in VULs are an investment and care must be taken in choosing which mutual funds are the best for you. We will discuss investing in mutual funds more thoroughly in the next chapter. There are risks associated with all investments and it is so important to understand the risks prior to any investing.

A nice thing about a VUL is that the mutual funds are growing tax-deferred, like a retirement account, meaning you do not have to pay any taxes on the growth of your account. You can also "borrow" the money from the separate account for any reason and at any time. The borrowed money can be used for retirement income, college education, vacations, room additions, anything – and never has to be paid back, because the money that is borrowed would just be taken out of the total death benefit when you died.

VULs became very popular during the Dot-Com Bubble period in the late 1990's because the mutual funds in the separate accounts were doing so well and no taxes had to be paid. However, when the bubble burst, the VULs came crashing down as well. There must be a certain investment or dollar amount in the separate account to keep the insurance in force.

So when the mutual funds went way down in value in the years

2000 - 2002, the insurance companies were asking for more money. People could not or did not want to come up with the amount and the policy lapsed, which resulted in no more insurance for the family. This obviously gave VULs a bad name. But a VUL can be a great product for the right people. They just have to be able to contribute much more than the minimum premium due. By contributing more they don't have to rely on the performance of the mutual funds so much to keep the policy in force.

A universal life policy, or UL, has a separate account that has a "fixed" investment attached to it. This separate account will have a guaranteed rate of return. These can be a good product for people who do not want the risks associated with mutual funds, but want the benefits of a separate account in a life insurance policy (money grows tax-deferred and can be withdrawn at any time for any reason). The "fixed" interest rate in the separate account varies for each insurance company; however, it is currently around 3% to 5% for most companies.

Permanent life insurance has a fixed premium, or payment amount, that depends on the amount of the death benefit, the sex of the insured, the age, and the health of the individual applying for life insurance. It will be the same amount for the rest of your life. The VUL (variable universal life) and the UL (universal life policy) premium includes the cost of insurance *and* the separate account or investment. You are allowed to put in more than the premium amount and the difference goes directly into the mutual funds or separate account, which I highly recommend if you go with these types of life insurance.

The IRS has now put limits on the amount of money that can go in based on the amount of the life insurance death benefit, because the VULs were being abused when they first started. Since there was no contribution limit, wealthy people were putting in tens of thousands of dollars extra and having it grow tax-deferred. The rich people were also taking the money out tax-free as a "loan" because they were "borrowing" the money. The IRS did not like this and fixed that problem by putting contribution limits on these types of life insurance policies.

Depending on how well the separate accounts perform in the life insurance policy, there could be a time when they might be able to pay your premium payments for you. So later in life you can have the separate accounts pay your premiums and you still have life insurance till the end of your life. It is important to monitor the separate account balance, just like any investment, because you do not want the policy to lapse because of lack of funds in the separate account.

There are still some companies that sell permanent life insurance called whole life or straight life policies. The death benefits are much lower because they are intended to pay off the immediate needs of the beneficiaries. These needs are funeral expenses, debt, and possibly time off work to try to adjust to the new unpleasant lifestyle. Sometimes they are called "burial policies" because that is usually what the amount will cover.

A major benefit to the permanent type of life insurance is the tax-deferred growth in the separate accounts, also called "cash value." The VUL and UL have their separate accounts and the whole life policies have what are called dividends that the insurance company pays to the insured. You can use the dividends to buy more life insurance, pay towards your current premiums, or have a check mailed to you.

The death benefit of life insurance goes to the beneficiaries and the cash value can go to you, if you want it or need it. I call the cash value the "living benefit" and it can be used for any reason. That is why I believe most people should have some form of permanent life insurance in their financial planning. It is there for your *family* if you die today and it is there for *you* if you live to be 100 years old.

The younger and healthier you are, the cheaper the life insurance premiums. As a young adult, if you can afford even a small permanent policy and put it in your budget, you could be better off in retirement years because of the tax-deferred growth in the separate accounts or mutual funds. You would also have much more in the cash value that could be used if you had an unfortunate catastrophe *during* your lifetime. But this should not be the only reason to buy this type of life insurance. The first and foremost reason is to protect the income of the wage earner, not because of the tax-deferred growth.

As you recall the graph about the amount of life insurance a person needs in their lifetime, it is important to know that you may have more than one policy at a time. You rent term insurance and you own permanent insurance. However, they work very well together. For example, a young couple starting out may purchase a 30-year term policy and a few years later are able to afford a permanent policy. When the 30-year term runs out and the need for the life insurance protection is much lower, they still have some coverage for the rest of their lives with the permanent policy. The permanent policy has the potential to continue to grow because of the cash value. If the need goes up again because of estate and death taxes, you will have some life insurance available for your beneficiaries to use to pay these taxes.

For a case in point, let's say you have a $500,000 thirty year term policy that started when you where 30 years old. This policy will end when you are 60 years old, right? Now at age 40, you are making more money and you find in your budget that you can afford a permanent type of life insurance. Some companies allow you to "convert" portions of your existing term life insurance into a permanent policy without any more underwriting.

In this example, say you want to convert $200,000 into a permanent policy. The term policy becomes less expensive because of the lesser death benefit amount, now only $300,000 and you now have a permanent policy for $200,000 for a total death benefit of $500,000 still. At age 60 the term policy ends and the amount of life insurance needed is less, but you still have a death benefit of $200,000 for the rest of your life, *plus* whatever the cash value/separate accounts has built up to.

There are other ways to use life insurance besides protecting the income of the wage earner, for example:

* ***Instant wealth creation*** – If you buy a $250,000 permanent policy, you just increased your "estate" by a quarter of a million dollars, which is that much more to pass on to beneficiaries and charities, and in most cases is tax-free to them.

* ***Give a large donation*** – You can make a non-profit organization or your home church the beneficiary of your life insurance.

* ***Home mortgage protection*** – Purchase a term policy on your life for the amount you owe on your home for the same amount of years on the mortgage.

I did not always feel so positive about life insurance. When I was a retail store owner and had equity in several businesses, I did not see a need for life insurance because I thought my family would be taken care of by the income of the businesses. Or they could just sell my half and live happily ever after.

But I reluctantly purchased life insurance on my wife and me anyway. In my opinion, life insurance was a scam, because term insurance runs out before you die and whole life was expensive for the amount the family received for the death benefit. They would pay for 30, 40, and 50 years to get a check for a whopping $10,000! One kind of life insurance didn't work and the other one was a rip-off! No one ever explained to me the value of protecting my income for my family.

It wasn't until I became a financial planner that I learned to appreciate all the incredible benefits of life insurance. But it took a long time to accept it. I really struggled with this paradigm shift, because I was so prejudiced and did not want to admit I was wrong.

When I delivered a check to a 25-year-old man in the amount of $250,000 I finally realized the significance of life insurance. I wasn't even the advisor for this family. This account had just been assigned to me because the original representative had retired. The first time I met the son, I gave him a check for a quarter of a million dollars. If this young man is a good steward with this money and still works hard, he will be financially stable for the rest of his life. If he is blessed with children later, their education and financial well-being might also be taken care of. This deceased single mother left an inheritance to her children's children.

There are two ways to determine the amount of life insurance a person needs. One is called "cash needs analysis" and the other way is called "human life value."

The cash needs analysis approach is to try to figure out what *all* the cash or income the family would need if the wage earner should die. For example: funeral expenses, mortgage, car loans, any other debt, children's education, spouse's education, what the income needs are today now that everything else has been paid, what the income needs are for the future, and possibly any estate taxes there might be when the second spouse dies.

If the other spouse who stayed at home and raised the children had died (not the principle wage-earner), then the needs would be different. There might be childcare issues, nannies, babysitters, or house-cleaners. So this "need" would be calculated, also. A good sound life insurance plan would include both parents.

At any rate, the cash needs analysis is a painstaking way of determining the amount of life insurance a person needs, especially since, in most cases, nobody wants to talk about it in the first place. The main problem with cash needs analysis is that the needs change over time. A different home, a job or career change, more dependants, any number of things could change.

A simpler and just as effective approach is the "human life value." You just multiply your annual income by twelve and that is how much life insurance that person needs. For example, a man earning $50,000 a year would need a policy for $600,000. A stay at home parent with no income still has incredible value to the family, obviously. I recommend about $300,000 for this person.

The reason for this approach is the reason for life insurance in the first place – it will replace the income of the wage earner. Let me explain. In the above example, if the wage earner dies, the beneficiaries would receive $600,000 net (life insurance proceeds goes to the beneficiaries tax-free in most cases). If this money was invested properly, it might produce anywhere from $35,000 to $50,000 a year in income and still have over a half million dollars in equity to use however the Lord leads in the future. It cannot replace the deceased of course, but it has replaced the income.

The other way to use the death benefit from the life insurance policy is to pay off the mortgage and other debts and then have lower monthly expenses. The balance of the death benefit would still be invested earning an income doing it this way. But, because a lot of the money went to paying off the mortgage, there would not be as much to invest, which means a lower dollar amount coming into the household. Also, most of your equity would be in the home and would not be as "liquid," meaning it is not as easy to get to if you need a large amount of money.

I mentioned a stay at home parent needing life insurance, because to replace what they do would take additional caregivers. The death benefit invested might earn about $20,000 a year and this could be used to pay for a nanny, or daycare, or whoever you choose to help raise your family so you are able to continue to earn a living or income.

Most people are underinsured. Most people do not understand the importance of life insurance in their financial planning. Most people do not see the value of life insurance, because it is something you buy not for yourself, but for the ones you love. Most people have heard the good, bad, and ugly stories of life insurance and are confused.

There are many options available and that is why it is essential to seek wise council, pray, and find a good financial advisor. Interview a couple and find one you are comfortable with who has excellent references. This person should have the same family values as you and your family. This is the person who will be there for you when there is a death in the family, who is not just looking for a "sale."

I've mentioned beneficiaries a couple of times already and will discuss this again in the Preservation or estate planning section. However, I want to mention here that I believe you should tithe when you are alive and you should tithe when you die. On the beneficiary section on the life insurance application, leave 10% to your home church and *then* decide how you want to distribute the rest.

If you already have life insurance and like this idea, have your insurance company send you a *change of beneficiary* form and make the appropriate changes. You will need the tax identification number of your church to do this correctly. Can you see how this could strengthen the church? Send out more short-term missionaries? Feed more hungry people? Give blankets to the homeless? Just doing one little thing in your financial planning can have eternal consequences and protect your family's future at the same time.

A quick note about the options that are available in life insurance policies, such as child riders, spouse riders, waiver of premium, and accidental death. We already talked about the child rider and its possible use. The spouse rider is similar to the child rider but with a larger death benefit and can be used in place of an individual policy on the spouse. This can work if you cannot afford a policy on the spouse or if she or he is potentially uninsurable.

Waiver of premium means that if you're disabled the insurance company will pay for your insurance during your disability. Some companies have excellent waiver of premium riders, and this should be considered.

The accidental death benefit can work well with younger persons, because most likely, if they die it will be because of accidents and not illnesses. My problem with accidental death benefits is that they have a lot of restrictions on the payouts, so be careful if you go that route and read all the fine print. I have never added this rider to a life insurance policy.

The appropriate insurance plan will protect the family, and that is what it is intended to do. There should not be too much insurance, which might cause the beneficiaries not to value hard work, but not too little which leaves the family destitute if the wage earner dies.

Some people are aware of the necessity of life insurance, but many neglect disability income insurance when determining their protection needs. Disability insurance helps replace lost income because of an accident or illness.

About 40% of all people aged 45 will experience a long term disability (at least 90 days) before they reach age 65. Over the course of a disability, you'll likely have an increase in expenses *and* a decrease in income, and that is a recipe for financial disaster.

Employer benefits that offer long term disability are the best way to go, because this is great coverage for the lowest price. The coverage, along with Social Security, usually pays 60% of your pre-tax income. It will never pay 100% of your income, because no one would get better if that was the case.

If it is not offered at work and you want an individual long term disability policy, here are a few things to keep in mind:

* **Purchase a non-cancelable policy**. The insurance company must insure you as long as you pay the premiums. It cannot be cancelled for any other reason and the premium can't be raised.

* **The policy must have cost-of-living adjustments**. This will ensure your benefits keep pace with inflation.

✳ **Make sure your policy does not differentiate between sickness and injury**. It does not matter to your checkbook whether you cannot work because you are injured or because you are sick.

The second of the three parts of protection in the Lord's Financial Plan is the protection against a liability. The dictionary says that *"liability* means to be liable or responsible, according to the law and being *exposed* to some adverse action." There are insurance products available to protect you against these adverse actions. Homeowner's, automobile, renters, boaters, and umbrella policies are the most common.

Another name for this type of protection is called property and casualty or P & C. These insurances protect you against loss of property in case of an accident, and protect you from a lawsuit. A judgment against you could result in the loss of everything you own and even your future earnings.

If you own a home or condominium, it is required by your lender to have adequate insurance coverage, so you do not walk away from your loan responsibility if some disaster happens like a fire. Even if your home is paid in full it still makes sense to have this protection. Homeowner's insurance protects your home, the structures attached to your home, and any unattached buildings that are not used for business purposes. It will also insure the items inside your home.

Most homeowner policies cover losses that are caused by fire, weight of snow and ice, explosions, aircraft and vehicles, smoke, windstorm, theft, riots, falling objects, vandalism, freezing of plumbing, and water leaks from plumbing.

Here is a list of what is *not* covered by homeowner's insurance: water damage caused by a flood, earthquake, mudslide, damage caused by deterioration or contamination, and damage caused by insects and animals. There is a separate coverage called earthquake insurance. It is expensive, has a high deductible, and does not insure very much. Some areas that are on a fault-line in the state require earthquake insurance. But if not required, I'd pass on this insurance.

There used to be a television commercial for an insurance company that said, "They will get you back to where you belong." It drove me crazy, because that is exactly what property and casualty insurance companies do, and they made it sound as if they were doing something special.

If your house caught on fire, the insurance company would fix it the way it was *before* the fire. However, there are additional riders or benefits that will allow you to meet the current inspection code if work is done on your home, but you cannot upgrade by adding a master suite, another bathroom, or another story, unless of course *you* want to pay for the difference.

Homeowner's insurance companies today have computer software that updates every year and *they* tell you how much insurance coverage you need for your home. That is not the case for your auto insurance, however. You and your car could do a lot more

---

You will be protected up to the amount of your liability coverage.

---

damage to others than your home could.

Your net worth [see your net worth statement done earlier] will determine how much protection you need from your auto insurance. This part is the liability section of auto insurance. On your insurance "declaration page," it is called Coverage A. This coverage pays to *other* people two possible amounts: 1) property damage and 2) personal injury, for which *you* are liable or responsible because of an auto accident. This would be for an auto accident where you were at fault.

If the other party does sue you, the liability coverage you have will pay for your insurance company's attorney, court costs, and claims. You will be protected up to the amount of your liability coverage. The property damage portion the other party will receive includes all damaged property and the *loss of use* of this property. So they will also get a rental car while their car is being repaired.

What the other party and their insurance company can *try* to collect on, *in addition* to the property damage you caused, is their personal injury amount. Personal injury is their medical expenses, pain and suffering, and any lost wages because of the accident caused by you. The personal injury amount can go up extremely high and very fast. This is where most of the protection is needed, because if not covered adequately, they can go after your assets and future income.

The collision coverage in automobile insurance pays for damages to *your* car in case of an accident, no matter who is at fault. A deductible is required for this coverage. The deductible is the amount you pay towards getting your own car fixed, even if it is someone else's fault. The higher the deductible, the lower the premiums. If your car is not worth very much, less than $2000, then this coverage is not an option for you, because the premiums don't justify the coverage.

The insurance companies usually determine what your car is worth by looking in the Kelly Blue Book. Many people believe they have not received fair market value for their car after an accident and have been completely frustrated by the experience. Perhaps you know someone who had their car paid off and then got in an accident, only to find the insurance company will give them an amount that cannot possibly replace their old car, and they now

The higher the deductible, the lower the premiums.

have to go finance a newer car and go into debt.

You need to have liability protection equal to your net worth, because if a lawsuit comes your way, the insurance company will pay the claim up to your coverage amount and you can keep your assets – they are protected. For example, if you have $100,000 equity in your home, $25,000 worth of personal property, and $25,000 in cash and investments, your net worth is $150,000. In this example, how much liability protection do you need? You are correct if you said $150,000. If you do not have enough liability protection, you are liable for the balance and the courts can go after your assets and income.

The highest automobile coverage amount you can get is $250,000, so what happens if your net worth is over this? The "umbrella" policy comes into play. Umbrella policies are sold in one million dollar increments and provide additional liability coverage to your existing P & C coverage. The insurance company makes you have the highest automobile and homeowners coverage amount before it will allow you to buy an umbrella policy, because if not, people would buy the lowest amount and have the remaining coverage on the less expensive umbrella policy.

It is called an umbrella policy because it covers you and your assets in almost all areas and it's extremely inexpensive for the protection it provides. Anyone with a net worth over $250,000 should have an umbrella policy. I recommend that most business owners have this protection because they can be so susceptible to lawsuits.

For example, your net total worth is $750,000 and you have a car accident and it is your fault, and you are found liable for the amount of $500,000. What happens? The automobile insurance will pay the first $250,000, and the umbrella policy kicks in and pays the balance of $250,000. Without the umbrella policy, you would have to come up with the remaining $250,000. Worse case scenario is having your wages or income garnished to pay the judgment.

Uninsured motorists' is additional coverage for your car. I am personally not an advocate of uninsured motorists' coverage. There are a few advantages, but not enough to pay for the higher premiums. P & C agents everywhere will be writing death threats to me as they read this.

Not all states require uninsured motorists coverage and the insurance company will make you sign a release for not getting it. The insurance agents will make you feel foolish for not having it, but it is double coverage. You are already protected without it.

I'll explain. If someone without auto insurance hits your car and it is damaged, *your* own collision coverage will repair your car minus your deductible amount. If an uninsured motorist hits your car and you are hurt, your own health insurance will provide for your medical care. Uninsured motorists' covers up to your deductible amounts and it will protect you if you are hit as a pedestrian. I don't think it's worth it.

Medical coverage on your automobile insurance is an extremely nominal coverage up to $3000. It is good only for the fact that there is not a deductible amount before this $3000. Medical coverage can be helpful to pay for the deductibles in your *own* personal health insurance if you are hurt in a car accident and need medical attention. This coverage does not cost very much because you don't receive very much.

A big question that almost everyone is unsure of is, "Who is covered and for what cars?" You, your spouse, and anyone else using your car *with your consent* are covered in most cases. If you rent a car or borrow a car, you are covered usually for up to 21 days. But a quick call to your agent will explain further, because not every insurance company is the same on this issue.

Homeowner's, auto, umbrella, and other P & C coverage insurance is protection of the assets God has entrusted us with and protection against lawsuits that could otherwise result in losing a portion of our future earnings. Sufficient planning in these areas is important and requires wisdom and discernment. We need to be adequately protected, but being careful to not be overly insured. That would be wasting money and not being a good steward.

There is one last section of protection in The Lord's Financial Plan, and that is having an emergency fund. An emergency fund is having three to six months' worth of expenses in an interest bearing account that you could access quickly. Because you now have a budget, you know how much three to six months' expenses are. As expenses change, so should the amount of your emergency fund. Having an emergency fund protects us from going back in debt.

This doesn't necessarily mean opening a savings account and labeling it "The Emergency Fund." Just having a sufficient amount of money in a bank or credit union savings account or in a money

---

Having an emergency fund protects us from going back in debt.

---

market account earning a small interest rate is good. In case of an emergency, you need cash quickly; it must not be tied up in a house or property requiring you to get a loan against it to get your needed emergency money.

Having a three to six month cushion is very helpful in case something major happens such as a job layoff or a serious medical situation in the family that might require time off from work. The reason you want an emergency fund is in case the transmission goes out in the car, the roof starts leaking inside your home or the washing machine finally dies. Having money available and easily accessible is another factor in enjoying the freedom you have created by getting out and staying out of debt.

On a lighter side, I also call the emergency fund the "The Good Deal Fund." How many times have you come across an incredible price on something and said, "Boy, if I only had the money?" In these instances, you could "borrow" the money from the emergency fund with the full intention of paying it back. Have there been times in the past where you would have liked to help someone financially? This fund could be the place. How about a friend or family member that needs seed money for a business, or expansion and you would like to be part of it? You could use your emergency fund.

People always ask me if it is OK to have their stock or mutual fund investments as an emergency fund. I tell them only if it is easily accessible and *if* there is an emergency, you *use* those investments and not go into debt. Because that is the main reason to have such an account – **to stay out of debt!**

The problems with a stock or mutual fund portfolio being used for your emergency fund is the capital gains taxes due to the IRS if the account has gone up in value. There also could be a "deferred sales charge" on the mutual funds sold, depending on the share class the mutual fund is in – this is explained in the next chapter. Stocks and mutual funds are usually a long-term investment and are not considered suitable for the liquidity needed for an emergency. This is why I think a bank or credit union savings or money market account works best.

One last note about an emergency fund is a little reminder of an earlier point I made regarding your auto insurance. The higher the deductible, the lower the premium. Keeping your deductibles at $500 or even $1000 will dramatically lower your premiums. Having money set aside in an emergency fund will allow you to self-insure for the first $500 or $1000.

I know a wonderful widowed missionary woman who is in her seventies. She and her husband travelled all over the world telling people about Jesus and were tremendous stewards of what God had blessed them with. She has a beautiful home with a swimming pool in a very nice hillside town. She has a well-thought-out plan to give to many charities after she passes away. She has a comfortable income and always has at least $40,000 in the bank.

She was so excited when she told me she had just saved money on her home and auto insurance by raising the deductibles! After all the work she had done in the previous months with her trust, her investments, the proper titles, and her charitable giving, she was more thrilled about saving $40 a month on her insurances. But I should have known, she still cleans the pool herself so she doesn't have to pay the pool guy.

I do not want anyone to get discouraged at this point. There is a lot of information and we are only in the beginning. It might seem like you will never get there, but remember, God is going to be faithful to you exponentially more when you are able to be obedient to Him. Give it all to Him and wait to see the wonders of God's grace and mercy.

> Isaiah 41:10 says: *Fear not, for I am with you: Be not dismayed, for I am your God. I will strengthen you, yes, I will help you, I will uphold you with My righteous right hand.*

No one can get everything we've discussed so far accomplished by this Tuesday at 7:30p.m. It takes time, patience, and obedience. It takes some people a few years to get to this point, but they do it right! And when it is time to move on to the second section of The Lord's Financial Plan, which is accumulation, they do that right, also.

> Proverbs 24: 27 *Prepare your outside work, make it fit for yourself in the field: and afterward build your house.*

Chapter 7 – Protection
Review Points

- Protection against loss of life, income, and going into debt is the place to start.

- Life insurance replaces the income of the wage earners.

- Stay-at-home parents need life insurance, also.

- Term insurance is for a period of time and is very affordable.

- Permanent insurance goes the whole life and is more costly.

- Multiply the annual income by 12 to determine how much life insurance is needed for primary wage earner.

- The liability protection amount for your automobile insurance should be equal to your total net worth.

- Create an emergency fund of 3 - 6 months worth of expenses (get number from the budget) in a liquid account like a money market for the purpose of staying out of debt.

Accumulation

John 6:27

Do not labor for the food which perishes, but for the food which endures to everlasting life, which the Son of Man will give you, because God the Father has set His seal on Him.

The second major section of the Lord's Financial Plan is the accumulation phase. After you have budgeted, eliminated debt, protected the family from disaster, is the time to start concentrating on accumulating assets, or *investing*. This is to get your money working for you through the power of compounding interest.

The great mathematician, Albert Einstein, once called compounding interest the Eighth Wonder of the World. We will discuss why it is so important to accumulate, what Jesus says about investing, and how and where are the best places to invest.

Before we begin, however, we must eliminate some negative myths regarding wealth. Poverty is not next to godliness. Being poor does not bring holiness any more than wealth brings sin.

God has used extremely rich people for His glory. Job, Abraham, David, and for a while Solomon (the richest man who ever lived) are examples in the Old Testament. Lydia, Lazarus, and Joseph of Arimathea in the New Testament were very wealthy people. In contemporary times, we learned of Penny, Heinz, Hershey, and Kellogg, to name a few. Perhaps you personally know wealthy people who have been used to glorify God with their wealth.

These people gave and shared their wealth and were incredible witnesses to God. Because of their stewardship of the gifts God gave them, the Gospel has been taken to the four corners of the globe. The wealthy do, however, have an *added* responsibility because of their gift of making money or having received a large inheritance. The Lord gives instructions to these people.

> 1 Timothy 6:17-19 says, *Command those who are rich in this present age not to be haughty, nor to trust in uncertain riches but in the living God who gives us richly all things to enjoy. Let them do good that they be rich in good works, ready to give, willing to share, storing up for themselves a good foundation for the time to come, that they may lay hold on eternal life.*

The Lord is more interested in our attitude about money. We are to make friends with the unrighteous mammon, to tame it so it does not control us. We tell our money where to go instead of wondering where it all went. Money is the least of all things. God wants us to have true riches, which are the intangible riches like love, joy and peace.

But first we must become good stewards — then He can work through us. He will only give us what we can handle. One day we will give an account to the Lord of what He has entrusted to us. So then why should we invest and accumulate wealth? **So that we are able to *give* more!** Why do we need to give more? **So that there will be an *equality* among us.**

This is God's PERFECT economic plan!

Paul, writing to the church in Corinth, says (and this needs to be read very slowly):

> 2 Cor. 8:12-15 *For if there is first a willing mind, it is accepted according to what one has, and not according to what he does not have. For I do not mean that others should be eased and you burdened; but by an equality, that now at this time your abundance may supply their lack, that their abundance also may supply your lack – that there may be equality. As it is written "He who gathered much had nothing left over, and he who gathered little had no lack."*

When people have abundance, and they give it to people who are lacking, there would be no want of any necessary item. Paul says in Romans that it is our *duty* to give. In the Old Testament, when the Israelites were starting to build the tabernacle, Moses asked for an offering. The people gave so much that they had to be restrained from giving. Moses gave a command to stop bringing an offering because they had more than enough.

> Exodus 36:6, 7 *Then Moses gave an order and they sent this word throughout the camp: "No man or woman is to make anything else as an offering for the sanctuary." And so the people were restrained from bringing more, because what they already had was more than enough to do all the work.*

Incidentally, 2 Corinthians 8:15 mentioned in the previous paragraph refers to Exodus 16:18, when the Lord provided Manna from Heaven in the morning, and quails in the evening. Every family had gathered according to each one's needs. Please go back and read chapter 16 in Exodus, it is very interesting. God will always provide what we need; it's our greed that He will not heed.

Jesus will always be our example and God's perfect economic plan is no exception. We give out of our abundance so we can ease the burdens of others who are less fortunate. In the same chapter in Corinthians verse 9, it explains how Jesus did this very thing for all Believers.

> *For you know the grace of our Lord Jesus Christ, that though He was rich, yet for your sakes He became poor, that you through his poverty might become rich.*

Jesus left all the glory, majesty, and riches that are rightfully His in Heaven to come down to earth in complete poverty to ease our burden of sin so we can have eternal life in Heaven. Our human mind cannot comprehend what Heaven looks like with the streets of gold, crystal seas, thrones like emeralds, walls of precious stones, angels singing "Holy, Holy, Holy," and the Glory of God illuminating it so much there is no need of a sun or moon. Jesus willingly gave all that up so we can experience that someday, *forever*. Jesus came as a newborn baby to a carpenter and his teenage betrothed fiancé and then died not owning anything but the robe off His back. He became destitute so we can become wealthier than our minds can understand or fully appreciate.

There is a saying that says, "Christians are so Heavenly minded that they are no earthly good." I disagree. I think if we *did* think more of Heaven we would become even *more* effective for the Lord.

In the Book of Acts, Paul is giving instructions to the elders of the church of Ephesus on his last and final time with them. He talks about many items during this meeting, but the last thing he says to them is in chapter 20 verse 35:

> *I have shown you in every way, by laboring like this,*

that you must support the weak. And remember the words of the Lord Jesus, that he said, "It is more blessed to give than to receive."

In Romans 12:3-8 Paul tells us to serve God with our spiritual gifts and to use them according to the grace that's given. Paul lists the gift of giving as one of these gifts. If some in the Body of Christ or church have this particular gift, then it stands to reason that God would equip those people to develop this gift.

As believers in Jesus Christ, we have the Holy Spirit living in us. Therefore, we all have spiritual gifts given to each and every one of us. Below is a list of all the spiritual gifts and where they are located in the New Testament.

The Lord has gifted us in different ways to fulfill the work of

Roman 12:6-8	1 Cor. 12:8-10	1 Cor. 12:28-30	Eph. 4:11	1 Peter 4: 9-11
Prophesy	Word of Wisdom	Apostleship	Apostleship	Speaking
Serving	Word of Knowledge	Prophesy	Prophesy	Serving
Teaching	Faith	Teaching	Evangelism	
Exhortation	Healings	Miracles	Pastor/Teacher	
Giving	Miracles	Healing		
Leading	Prophesy	Administrating		
Showing mercy	Discerning of Spirits	Tongues		
	Tongues	Interpretation of Tongues		
	Interpretation of Tongues			

the Body of Christ. Each one of us has one, two, sometimes even three dominant gifts. We have *all* the gifts in us; it is just that we are more empowered with certain ones.

For example, my main gift is administration or organization. I am an organized freak! Everything has a place – everything in its place. I don't even have a junk drawer in the kitchen, everything is in order. Even *looking* at an unorganized desk or garage disturbs me.

Giving and speaking are other dominant gifts that God has given to me. Now I have the gift in me of showing mercy – it is however, not very powerful. I have prayed many times for the Lord to allow me to develop all the spiritual gifts, but I will always have my main gifts that are magnified greater than the other gifts.

This is true for every believer. This is why the Body of Christ can be so effective, unique, and mighty. It is our responsibility to find and know our spiritual gifts. Pray and ask God to show you the very special gifts He has given to you, so you may use them for His glory.

Rick Warren's awesome book, "The Purpose Driven Life" explains how you can know your spiritual gifts and use them for your personal ministry within the church and your mission to unbelievers outside the church. He uses the acronym S.H.A.P.E. to know your giftedness.

S **Spiritual Gifts** – know what they are.

H **Heart** – your passion in life and to serve God with all your heart.

A **Abilities** – what we are *able* to do and *capable* of doing.

P **Personalities** – determining how and where you will use your gifts.

E **Experiences** – families, education, vocation, spiritual, even painful experiences help to determine our particular spiritual gifts.

Let's get back to The Lord's Financial Plan and how it relates

---

We actually *develop* the gift of giving by giving.

---

to God's perfect economic plan. We accumulate or invest so we are able to give more, and when we give more there is equality among people. We actually *develop* the gift of giving *by* giving. Paul explains this phenomenon to the church in Corinth.

> 2 Cor. 9:6-15 *But this I say: He who sows sparingly will also reap sparingly, and he who sows bountifully will also reap bountifully. So let each one give as he purposes in his heart, not grudgingly or of necessity; for God loves a cheerful giver. And God is able to make all grace abound toward you, that you, always having all sufficiency in all things, may have an abundance for every good work. As it is written: "He has dispersed abroad, He has given to the poor; His righteousness endures forever." Now may He who supplies seed to the sower, and bread for food, supply and multiply the seed you have sown and increase the fruits of your righteousness, while you are enriched in everything for all liberality, which causes thanksgiving through us to God. For the administration of this service not only supplies the needs of the saints, but also is abounding through many thanksgivings to God, while, through the proof of this ministry, they glorify God for the obedience of your confession to the gospel of Christ, and for your liberal sharing with them and all men, and by their prayer for you, who long for you because of the exceeding grace of God in you. Thanks be to God for His indescribable gift!*

I love verse 8, *and God is able to make **all** **grace** abound toward you, that you, **always having all sufficiency** in **all things**, may have an abundance for **every good work**.*

That is one of my favorite promises in all of scripture. That is how God gives to us. God is a giver and He wants us to be like Him. We cannot outgive God. The more we give, the more God gives to us. The more God gives to us, the more thankful we become. The more thankful we become, the more righteous we get. The more righteous we get, the more we give. The more we give... A perfect giving cycle created by a perfect God.

What does Jesus say about accumulating? Please read the following familiar Parable of the Talents, taking it all in. Then I will explain how, in this parable, Jesus actually gives us a command to invest. This is Jesus talking to His disciples in Math. 25: 14-30.

> *For the kingdom of Heaven is like a man traveling to a far country, who called his own servants and delivered his goods to them. And to one he gave five talents, to another two, and to another one, to each according to his own ability; and immediately he went on a journey. Then he who had received the five talents went and traded with them, and made another five talents. And likewise he who received two gained two more also. But he who had received one went and dug in the ground, and hid his lord's money.*
>
> *After a long time the lord of those servants came and settled accounts with them. So he who had received five talents came and brought five other talents, saying, "Lord, you delivered to me five talents; look, I have gained five more talents besides them."*
>
> *His Lord said to him, "Well done, good and faithful servant; you were faithful over a few things, I will*

make you ruler over many things. Enter into the joy of your lord."

Verse 22 *He also who had received two talents came and said, "Lord, you delivered to me two talents; look, I have gained two more talents besides them." His lord said to him, "Well done, good and faithful servant; you have been faithful over a few things, I will make you ruler over many things. Enter into the joy of your lord." Then he who received the one talent came and said, "Lord, I knew you to be a hard man, reaping where you have not sown, and gathering where you have not scattered seed. And I was afraid, and went and hid your talent in the ground. Look, there you have what is yours." But his lord answered and said to him, "You wicked and lazy servant, you knew that I reap where I have not sown, and gather where I have not scattered seed. So you ought to have deposited my money with bankers, and at my coming I would have received back my own with interest. Therefore take the talent from him, and give it to him who has ten talents. For to everyone who has, more will be given, and he will have abundance; but from him who does not have, even what he has will be taken away. And cast the unprofitable servant into the outer darkness. There will be weeping and gnashing of teeth."*

Verse 15 says how the man distributed his goods to his servants – *to each according to his own ability.* Isn't that encouraging? We are not all created to be financial wizards. We all have different abilities and gifts and we all have different degrees of aptitudes, especially in our finances. The Lord does expect us to use our gifts to the *best* of our ability though, because that glorifies Him.

In this parable, the first man was extremely good in handling money, investments, and business. We know this because he was the only servant who *traded with them*. The man who left to travel was also being a good steward because he gave to his servants each according to their own ability. He would've made a big mistake if he had reversed the order and given the most to the lazy servant. The first servant must have proven himself worthy previously to be entrusted with two and a half times more than the others.

The second servant gained two talents. He doubled the investment – just like the first servant. Maybe the second servant didn't have the business acumen or the trading ability in the marketplace as the first servant. But guess what? They both earned the same returns on their investment and they were both rewarded the same, minus one talent (verse 28).

The last servant, who buried the money, was rebuked and cast into outer darkness where there will be weeping and gnashing of teeth – OUCH! I've always felt this punishment was extreme; however, God can do what He wants with His creation. It also shows how serious God takes our stewardship over what He has given us. This servant has a history of poor stewardship. He only received one talent because he was given according to his own ability. He then proves to his master that he was not even worthy of the one talent.

The master calls the last servant, "wicked and lazy." The Book of Proverbs has quite a lot to say about the destructiveness of laziness.

> Proverbs 10:4, 5 *He who has a slack hand becomes poor, but the hand of the diligent makes rich. He who gathers in summer is a wise son; He who sleeps in harvest is a son who causes shame.*

It does not matter what our level of knowledge in the area of finances is. The Lord does expect multiplication and not just maintenance, because the lord tells the last servant he should have at least deposited the money with the bankers to earn some interest. If you are not gifted in this area, then put your money in a bank or credit union's C.D. (Certificate of Deposit) and earn *something*. This can be the best form of stewardship for many people. As we prove our trustworthiness, the Lord will entrust more to us.

I have taught on this parable many times and there are many incredible truths and applications to this story. But I had missed something very important that kind of bewilders me, though it really shouldn't because God's Word can never be completely understood while we are still on earth. At any rate, verse 19 has the key words to accumulation or investing: *After a long time...*

Proper accumulation of assets does take a long time. It is not a "get rich quick" way of thinking. It takes patience, perseverance, and persistence. Yes, the first two servants doubled their money *after a long time,* and they were rewarded for their stewardship.

We don't know, but maybe the last servant was given only one talent because of his history of blown opportunities, or his get rich quick mindset. Maybe he was afraid of losing the money on a bad "deal" and he feared the master's wrath. The bank's interest rate wasn't very attractive to him so the best option to him was to bury it in the ground and gain nothing.

I can almost feel the bitterness in this servant's voice, "He only gave me one – I'll show him. I won't do anything." He does nothing and loses everything. Could his pride have gotten in the way? "I only received one, what can I do with one?" Even with little resources, *after a long time* in a conservative investment like a bank or credit union C.D., the money will grow and you *will* be rewarded for your stewardship.

We now know the Lord wants us to invest. But how do we do it? Let's look at the "perfect investment" and its characteristics.

✱ Very high rate of return

* No taxes due, keep everything you earn
* Safe, can't lose anything
* Liquid, get it when you want it
* No financial knowledge required, put money in and "let it ride"

Unfortunately, this investment does not exist. However, there are several investment vehicles to choose from. Since there are no perfect investments, you want the *best* vehicles for you and your family. By answering the following questions, you would narrow your choices down considerably and with praying and seeking wise counsel, you will end up with the best choice or choices for you.

1) What are my goals for this investment?
Is it for current income? Is it to save for my retirement? Is it for my children or grandchildren's college education? Is it to save for a big purchase like a home? Why am I investing this money?

2) How liquid should it be (investment into cash)?
When do I need the money? Is this a short term or long term investment? How easy is it to get to?

3) What is my risk tolerance?
How much risk can I handle? Higher risk = higher reward, lower risk = lower reward (I have included a questionnaire at the end of the chapter to help determine your personal risk tolerance.)

4) What is the impact of taxes and inflation?
"Qualified" accounts, like an IRA, grow tax-deferred, meaning you do not pay taxes on the growth; you "qualify" for this benefit by the IRS's retirement plans. Non-qualified investments might have taxes due every year because of dividends and capital gains. And inflation averages almost 3% a year. How will this affect my "total return"?

5) How much skill and knowledge do I need?
Do I need professional advice? Can I do this by myself? How much time can I put into gaining knowledge for my investments?

6) How much can I invest?
What is the amount I can put away every month comfortably? Or is it a lump sum, like an inheritance or a rollover from a company retirement plan?

Albert Einstein invented the Rule of 72. This is a mathematical formula that helps you to determine how many years it will take to double your investment at a specific rate of return. You can do this by dividing the rate of return earned into the number 72 and the answer is how long it will take for your money to double.

Unless your investment is in a "fixed" account and earning the same interest every year, you would never have exact returns. But you can find the historical return of an investment and the Rule of 72 would give you an idea of what to possibly expect in the future.

Rate of Return	1%	2%	3%	4%	6%	8%	10%
Years to double	72	36	24	18	12	9	7.2
Years to triple	115	57.5	38.3	28.8	19.2	14.4	11.5

However, past performance is not indicative of future results.

The Rule of 115 is a similar rule in finding out how many years it will take for your investment to *triple* in value. Do this by dividing the rate of return into 115 and that tells you in years.

Oh, the power of compounding interest!

Here is some information on the tools of accumulation.

Stocks: A stock refers to a fractional ownership of a corporation. Also known as equities, stocks may be traded in U.S. stock markets like the New York Stock Exchange, for example. Compared to other investments, stocks have historically produced the highest long-term returns, but generally experience the highest short-term volatility or risk.

Bonds: Bonds are "IOUs" issued by corporations or governments in exchange for your loan to them. Bond issuers promise to pay you interest on your loan and to repay the principal amount of the loan itself on a specific maturity date. Bonds are considered less risky than stocks.

Mutual Funds: A share is a combination of stocks or bonds in a large portfolio managed by a money manager who has a specific investment objective, such as growth, income, value, or international. The best way to have a diversified portfolio is with mutual funds, and you can start with as little as $25.

Life Insurance: Mentioned earlier about the benefits of tax-deferral and long-term growth potential in a cash-value type of policy.

Annuities: Investments that are issued by life insurance companies. Also a good tax-deferral strategy that allows you to be invested in mutual funds. The downside to these types of investments is the "surrender" charge for premature withdrawal. Similar to retirement accounts, such as an IRA and 401(k), in that the money cannot be touched before the age of 59½ without a 10% federal penalty.

Savings Accounts: Money in a bank, credit union, or savings and loan that earns a small interest on money invested

Investment Pyramid

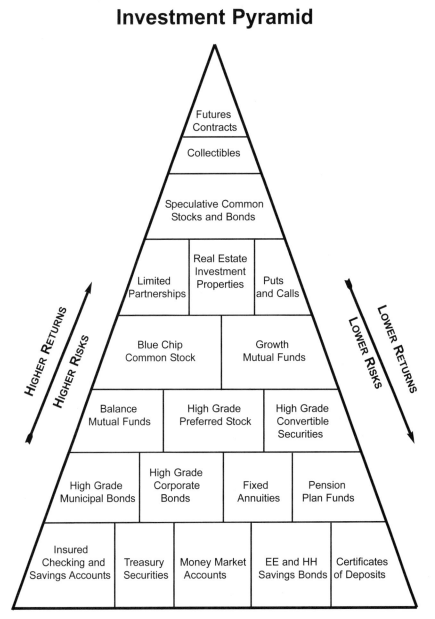

This is just a list of the types of investments that are available and is not a recommendation for any specific investment. Because the risks, returns, and degree of safety of any investment varies, even on the same pyramid level, you should consult a qualified financial planner before making any investment.

and these are very safe and liquid.

Money Market: Similar to savings accounts except can earn higher interest but sometimes require higher balances.

C.D's/Certificates of Deposits: Money in a bank, credit union, or savings and loan for a specific period of time, such as 12, 18, 24 months, that earns a fixed interest. These are guaranteed by the banking institution and have virtually no risk.

Real Estate: The most popular investment with some tax benefits. A great way to accumulate wealth, but also the least liquid.

I always recommend to people their employer's retirement plans as the first place to invest, if that is available, and especially if the company will also contribute money into the account. You cannot beat free money! Put in as much as you can because it is essentially a "write-off" on your income. You do not pay income tax on the amount going into the plan *and* the amount is growing tax-deferred *and* the company is putting money into your account. What a great deal!

Tax-deferred means the earnings your investments accumulate are free from any taxation until you withdraw the money. Now when you retire or leave the company, you would then rollover your employer's plan into your own individual retirement account or IRA. You can access the money after the age of 59½ without a penalty. Prior to this age, most withdrawals would have a 10% penalty from the IRS.

Company sponsored plans are called 401(k)'s, 403(b)'s, or 457, and these numbers represent the address in the enormous IRS tax code. All of these can be rolled over into an IRA when you leave the company or retire. The final resting place for all company plans should be in an IRA. The reasons for this are you will have much more investment options available and you have more control. If a catastrophe should happen you could access the money in an IRA,

How a Traditional IRA Works

Account Owner

* Contribution may be tax deductible.

* Total Annual contribution is limited.

* Annual contribution limits are coordinated with any Roth IRA.

IRA Account

* May be opened anytime between January 1 of current year until due date of tax return.

* Earnings accumulate tax deferred.

* Account is usually self-directed (participant controls investments).

* A separate spousal IRA may be established for a spouse with little or no earned income.

Early Withdrawal

* A 10% penalty applies if withdrawals are made before age 59½.

* Some exceptions to 10% penalty are available.

* Earnings + deductible contributions are taxed as ordinary income in year received.

Retirement

* Distributions must begin by April 1 of year following year owner reaches age 70½.

* Required minimum distribution rules apply.

* Earnings + deductible contributions are taxed as ordinary income in year received.

Death

* Value of IRA is included in owner's gross estate.

* Proceeds can pass to surviving spouse, with payments made over survivor's lifetime.

* Income and estate taxes can severely reduce IRA funds left to non-spousal beneficiaries.

whereas you might not be able to in a company plan.

IRA stands for Individual Retirement Account. It is for an individual who earned income and wants to make contributions in a retirement account. The money that goes in, is an income tax deduction and the money grows tax-deferred. When you withdraw from an IRA, the money will be considered income and you will be taxed accordingly at your income tax rate. As in all retirement accounts there are limits to the amount of money that can go in every year.

Roth IRAs are also individual retirement accounts except the contributions going in every year are not considered income tax deductions. The investment still grows tax-deferred, but, when you withdraw money from a Roth IRA there is no income tax due. These are a great way to compliment your retirement planning by having some tax-free income coming into the household. You cannot rollover your company retirement plan into a Roth IRA, you can only rollover into a traditional IRA. The Roth IRA is named after the Republican Delaware Senator William Roth who sponsored it and it was approved in 1997.

Our government will allow us to write off our contributions going into retirement plans, because what they really want to tax is the whole retirement that comes out during the retirement years. Our government is extremely patient. They do not want to tax the seed being planted – they want to tax the whole harvest later on.

Social Security is going to be less and less of our retirement income and our retirement is going to be more and more our responsibility. Our government encourages savings in these accounts, because it will not be able to support people in the future like it has done in the past. So it is important that we know the tax-deferred strategies available to us.

Our government is able to do generous things because of taxes and it runs by the taxes that you pay. In the same way, the church is run by the tithing it receives and is able to change lives all over the world.

How a Roth IRA Works

Account Owner

* Contribution are not tax deductible.

* Total annual contribution is limited.

* Annual contribution limits are coordinated with any traditional IRA.

Qualified Distribtions

* Qualified distributions are tax-free if a five-year holding period is met and one of the following applies – The owner is over 59½, dies, becomes disabled or the distribution is for up to $10,000 of qualified first-time homebuyer expenses.

Roth IRA Account

* May be opened anytime between January 1 of current year and the due date of tax return.

* Traditional IRA can be converted to a Roth IRA

* Earnings accumulate tax-deferred.

* Account is usually self-directed (owner controls investments).

* A separate spousal Roth IRA may be established for a spouse with little or no earnings.

Retirement

* Assuming compensation, contributions may continue to any age.

* No mandatory age for starting withdrawals.

* No minimum distributions required while owner is alive.

* Qualified distributions are received free of federal income tax.

Death

* Value of Roth IRA is included in owner's federal gross estate.

* If five-year holding period is met, beneficiaries receive funds free of federal income tax.

* A surviving spouse may choose to treat an inherited Roth IRA as his or her own.

When the Pharisees tried to trick Jesus with the question, *"Tell us, therefore, is it lawful to pay taxes to Caesar, or not?" Jesus answered, "Pay therefore to Caesar the things that are Caesar's, and to God the things that are God's."* So we are to pay our tithes and we are to pay our taxes. We are not trying to cheat our government out of what is theirs. We are just trying to delay it as much as possible and be knowledgeable about the tax laws that the IRS writes and enforces.

The only other tax-deferral investments are life insurance policies, which have been explained earlier, and annuities. An annuity is either fixed or variable and it is also an insurance product. Fixed annuities give you a fixed rate of return on your investment. Variable annuities are invested in mutual funds and vary from day to day. The mutual funds in a variable annuity are registered as investments or securities with FINRA (the regulatory agency that oversees all investments and advisors that used to be the SEC and NASD), so the same thought process applies to the mutual fund choices and the risks associated as such. You can put as much as you want in an annuity, well, up to $1,000,000 in any one contract, and that limit is from the insurance company, not the government.

It is similar to a retirement plan, in that you would have a 10% penalty if you withdrew any money before the age of 59½ and the money grows tax-deferred.

There are some guarantees on annuities given by the insurance companies, which make the expenses higher than a regular mutual fund investment. I think the fees are sometimes worth it, to get the guarantees and tax deferral; yet, tax-deferral should not be the only reason to invest in an annuity.

The two types of guarantees that variable annuities offer are a death benefit guarantee and guaranteed income stream. When the owner of an annuity passes away, the money goes to their designated beneficiaries. Obviously the market fluctuates year to year and when the owner dies it's possible the market could be down from previous highpoints, like all investments.

If it is more important to pass on the investment than to use the money yourself, then you would buy a rider that guarantees the beneficiaries the highest anniversary value, which is based on the anniversary of the purchase date, *or* the current market value of the investment. Your beneficiary would receive the highest of the two; either the current value or the highest anniversary date's value.

If it is more important that you use this investment for an additional source of income, you can buy a rider that guarantees an income stream to you for the rest of your life and then your beneficiaries will still get the whole investment when you pass away. Some riders allow you to receive five percent of the balance of your investment, without ever touching the principle. For example, if your variable annuity investment was $100,000 – you would receive $416 a month for the rest of your life, and your investment is still invested and can go up or down, which will go to your beneficiaries when you pass away. You still have control of *your* money.

While insurance companies make a number of specific guarantees about the variable annuities and riders they offer, there is NO such guarantee applying to the investment return or to the principal. The principal can still LOSE value.

These newer types of guarantees have become very popular in the last couple of years and have helped many people increase their monthly income. In the past, you would have to "annuitize" to receive income and also lose all access to your money. It would be like a pension in that regard.

When I first started in the finance industry, I did not like annuities very much. I didn't understand them at all. They seemed so complicated with all these bells and whistles. Why not just go in regular mutual funds, was my thinking. However, after learning more about their value in tax-deferred wealth accumulation, guarantees for the transfer of money to the beneficiaries, and understanding the income they can produce, I realized they can be a great product for the right situation. But with that in mind, there are some absolutely horrific annuities out there! Here is a list of what to look for in an annuity:

1.) **Pay close attention to the surrender schedule and early withdrawal charges**. It does not cost anything to buy an annuity, 100% of your money is invested, so the insurance company wants to make sure the money stays invested for a few years or they charge a penalty. Make sure the length fits your financial goals.

2.) **The expenses for the annuity**. The annuity will have additional expenses over and above the mutual fund expenses inside the annuity. This is where the guarantees and riders come in. Make sure you understand what you are paying for.

3.) **The insurance company**. Guarantees are only as good as the company backing them. Make sure it is an "A" rated company. Even then, there is NO guarantee on the investment return in variable annuities. The principal can still lose value.

4.) **Sub-Account choices.** For variable annuities, the sub-accounts, or mutual funds, are still the driving force behind the investment. Make sure the mutual funds choices are many so you are able to make a portfolio that is suitable for you and your specific risk tolerance.

5.) **The advisor recommending the annuity**. Get referrals and information on the background of the advisor.

There are many factors in choosing the right investment for you and your family, and they should all be discussed and gone over thoroughly. Know what all your options are before making a decision. As in all important choices, pray and seek wise counsel.

I read an article a few years ago called *The 10 Most Common Retirement Mistakes* written by Stephan Leimburg and David

Cordell, which I enjoyed and agree with. I'll explain what they meant.

1.) "You depend on someone else"
Relying on Social Security and pension plans will not be enough. Take responsibility for your retirement. Start putting something away that will have the benefit of compounding over several years. Some people call this "the three-legged stool." You cannot sit in a chair with only one leg – Social Security. You cannot sit in a chair with only two legs – Social Security and a pension plan. You *can* sit on a stool with three legs – Social Security, pension plan, and personal investment like an I.R.A.

How does a rocking chair sound? This is multiple streams of income. Social Security, pension plan, Roth IRA, Traditional IRA, life insurance, miscellaneous investments like mutual funds, and even rental income from real estate. This is the freedom that being out of debt allows you to have, by allowing you to start investing. It all begins with proper stewardship.

2.) "You have a dream rather than a goal"
Most people have not thought enough about their retirement years. "I want to travel" or "I just want to be comfortable" is too vague. These are dreams. You need a goal. "By the time I reach 65 years old, I want an income of $50,000 a year for the remainder of my life that will be adjusted for inflation." This is a quantitative goal. Begin now to figure out what you will need to have accumulated to reach your goal. Advisors or the internet can help with this equation.

If you are in a position where you are self-sufficient financially and don't have to work any more at a career, imagine the ministry or ministries you can be part of! If you want to travel, you can serve the Lord on short-term missionary trips. If you want to be comfortable in your own home, then disciple someone or grade Bible studies for prisoners. Believers never truly retire.

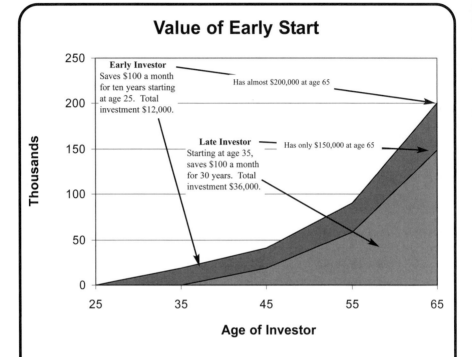

Value of Early Start

Early Investor
Saves $100 a month for ten years starting at age 25. Total investment $12,000.

Has almost $200,000 at age 65

Late Investor Has only $150,000 at age 65
Starting at age 35, saves $100 a month for 30 years. Total investment $36,000.

Thousands (y-axis: 0, 50, 100, 150, 200, 250)

Age of Investor (x-axis: 25, 35, 45, 55, 65)

An **Early Investor** who saves $100 a month for ten years starting at age twenty-five and then leaves the money invested will have approximately $200,000 when he or she retires at age 65.

A **Late Investor** who saves $100 a month for thirty years starting at age thirty-five will only have roughly $150,000 at age 65. The late investor will have invested $36,000 dollars whereas the early investor will have invested only $12,000.

To have $200,000 at age 65, a Late Investor would have to invest:

    ✱ $135 a month (or $48,000 total) starting at age 35
    ✱ $340 a month (or $81,600 total) starting at age 45
And a whopping
    ✱ $1095 a month (or $131,400 total) starting at age 55

These numbers assume an average 8% return on their investment.

3.) "You don't invest"

People get in debt so early in life that they can never get started. Any extra money goes to pay bills, and nothing is left over to invest. Save *something* every month and invest it. A rule of thumb for years has been to put away 10% of your income in an investment – "pay yourself first." As Christians, we should give God 10%, save 10%, and learn to live on 80%.

4.) "You start too late"

This one is similar to the last mistake, in that most people cannot get started. Worse yet, most people don't even think about their retirement income until it's too late. Starting later means you lose the power of compounding interest, and then you have to invest even more because there aren't as many years. Do not let this deter you, please. The best time to plant an oak tree was 100 years ago; the next best time is NOW.

5.) "You fail to insure your plan"

We have already talked about this in the protection section. Nothing will ruin your retirement plan faster than a premature death. Disability, accident, or a lawsuit will be a financial nightmare unless you have proper protection or insurance in place.

6.) "You don't take into account taxes and inflation"

Take advantage of tax-deferred investments as much as you can. These are company sponsored retirement plans, IRAs, annuities, and cash-value type of life insurances. You will be taxed when you take the money out, at your then current income tax level, however, the taxes are usually less because you are retired and not earning as much income so you are in a lower tax bracket.

Unless, of course, you been an excellent steward for a long time, and the Lord has blessed you and your investments, and your income from these investments puts you in a higher tax bracket. If this is the case, then you will want to invest a portion in municipal bond mutual funds, because you do not pay federal income tax on the dividends. If you invest in your state's municipal bond mutual funds, then you will not pay state income tax, either.

7.) "You expect someone else to do your thinking for you"

Many people blindly trust others with their money. They do not want to take the time to learn the fundamentals of money management. CPAs are a great example of how much people trust them. Accountants take their responsibility as money gatekeepers for their clients very seriously and they are to be commended. But it still amazes me how many people believe their CPA or accountant is the All-Powerful Financial Guru, and they listen to every word like it is Scripture. Accountants are extremely important when it comes to year-end taxes, filings, and the enormous amount of tax laws they need to stay current on; however, doing that alone is a full-time job.

They do not have the time or resources to know all there is to know in the investment and insurance world and to stay current on all the compliance issues. Financial advisors, estate attorneys, and CPAs make a great team because each does his job full time and is an expert in his field. One of my favorite mottos is "Let the expert do their expert thing." I tell people you don't want to buy a fish taco at a hamburger place.

Here is a word of caution while we are on this subject. Be extremely leery of anyone who sells financial products on a part-time basis. Mechanic by day and insurance by night. Very seldom do they have proper training to advise you correctly, unless of course they want to recruit you, then they will have all the training humanly possible.

The main trouble with this is that most of them will not be in the business two years from now, because they will not earn enough income to justify going to all their meetings. This industry is tough enough going all out full-time; trying to do it part-time just does not work for the majority who try.

I have helped a lot of people who said, "We trust you, just tell us what to do and we'll do it." I get to know these people better because I need to spend more time with them explaining their options and strategies, and that helps me to help them pursue their financial goals.

Sometimes I get there first and I am able to explain their choices and assist them. But what if a shady commission-starving wolf has talked them into some investment that was wrong for the client but excellent for the advisor? Unfortunately, this happens too many times.

This is going to sound like I am a traitor to the financial industry, but I believe a large percent of people are in it for the wrong reasons. This is true in every industry, but when you are dealing with someone's financial future, it makes it especially hard to swallow.

One of my clients wanted me to go visit her elderly mom and review her investments. This wonderful trusting German grandmother had previously responded to a postcard in the mail from a small investment company that claimed to specialize in the Senior Citizen market. When I reviewed what this so-called professional did to this grandma, it made me want to scream. He had liquidated two of her variable annuities from an "A" rated insurance company, and put her into two new "indexed" annuities.

The new annuities had a surrender schedule of 12 years and in the process cost this woman over $100,000 in death benefit value from the first two annuities that would have gone to her daughters and grandchildren. This is an example of some of the horrific annuities available that I mentioned earlier.

There was no reason at all to change her annuities. She didn't want the money, it was all for her family, part of her legacy. And he lost it for them, so he could make a commission. This wolf would not even talk to her when she called to ask him to explain this product to her again. I couldn't tell her that she had made a dreadful mistake. She trusted the wrong person.

8.) "You micromanage your portfolio"

I think we have all met someone who bought a *Money* magazine once and became Warren Buffet overnight. They make changes monthly, wanting to buy the hottest stock – buying and selling with no plan in place, and do not have the patience for steady growth. This is poor stewardship.

You want to develop a sound strategy for your investments, based on the answers to the questions earlier in the chapter. A well-diversified portfolio needs to be rebalanced every 3-6 months depending on the size of the investment. Have an annual or bi-annual review and see what is and what is not working, and then make the appropriate changes.

Here is my analogy of rebalancing. It is like an animal race.

* There is the turtle – slow and sure
* The cow – plods along all day
* The horse – gallops and runs and is strong
* And the cheetah – super fast for short bursts

When the race starts, all the animals are doing what they are supposed to. But after 3 to 6 months we have to blow the whistle and end the race because we have to start another race. We could exchange turtles, maybe the horse turned to glue during the race, and we know the cheetah is tired. So we might need different animals for the next 3 to 6 month race. The key to investing is to know your goals, diversify your portfolio, and rebalance regularly.

9.) "Your plan ends too soon"

Once *you* retire, your plan does not. You will need to shift your focus from a growth type of strategy to a more conservative model, from accumulation to conservation. You should be thinking about preserving the capital and possibly generating an income from your investments. The average person lives 17 years after retirement, and that number is going up every year. You need to continue to plan even after retirement.

10.) "You underestimate what it is going to take"

Another rule of thumb is 70% to 80% of your present income will give you the same lifestyle after you retire. However, this is shifting towards 90% to100% because of travel plans, medicines, and long-term care. Social security will provide some, a possible pension plan or profit sharing might provide more, but the rest is up to you.

Social Security is only one part of a successful retirement, but an important part. Each year Social Security sends your statement in the mail a couple of months before your birthday [see page 140]. I call it the Social Security birthday card, and it will tell you your projected benefits at various retirement ages. If you have a pension plan, you can call and request your projected pension benefits from your employer's human resource department. These are very important in determining how much you will need to have saved by your retirement date.

For example, if you earn $75,000 a year now, you will need about $60,000 in retirement income to maintain the same lifestyle, or $5000 a month. Let's say that your Social Security will be about $1600 and you have a pension plan that is estimated to give you $600 a month. You are still short $2800 a month, or $33,600 a year. You would have to have about $500,000 in investments so that you could live off the interest that is earning 6% to 8%. And this still does not consider inflation.

Run the numbers every year to make sure you are on track. A goal to have is to retire from your job so you can now work for the Lord full-time. You want to be free to serve Him and not have to worry about an income. Freedom!

This is one of my favorite Social Security stories. In 1940, Ida May Fuller of Vermont received the very first monthly Social Security check. Over three years she contributed a total of $24.75 to the program. Ida May lived to be 100 and received $22,888 in

Social Security Benefit Statement

▼ Your Estimated Benefits

To qualify for benefits, you earn "credits" through your work—up to four each year. This year, for example, you earn one credit for each $970 of wages or self-employment income. When you've earned $3,880, you've earned your four credits for the year. Most people need 40 credits, earned over their working lifetime, to receive retirement benefits. For disability and survivors benefits, young people need fewer credits to be eligible.

We checked your records to see whether you have earned enough credits to qualify for benefits. If you haven't earned enough yet to qualify for any type of benefit, we can't give you a benefit estimate now. If you continue to work, we'll give you an estimate when you do qualify.

What we assumed—If you have enough work credits, we estimated your benefit amounts using your average earnings over your working lifetime. For 2006 and later (up to retirement age), we assumed you'll continue to work and make about the same as you did in 2004 or 2005. We also included credits we assumed you earned last year and this year.

We can't provide your actual benefit amount until you apply for benefits. **And that amount may differ from the estimates stated below because:**
(1) Your earnings may increase or decrease in the future.
(2) Your estimated benefits are based on current law. **The law governing benefit amounts may change.***
(3) Your benefit amount may be affected by **military service, railroad employment or pensions earned through work on which you did not pay Social Security tax.** Visit *www.socialsecurity.gov/mystatement* **to see whether your Social Security benefit amount will be affected.**

Generally, estimates for older workers are more accurate than those for younger workers because they're based on a longer earnings history with fewer uncertainties such as earnings fluctuations and future law changes.

These estimates are in today's dollars. After you start receiving benefits, they will be adjusted for cost-of-living increases.

▼ ***Retirement**   You have earned enough credits to qualify for benefits. At your current earnings rate, if you stop working and start receiving benefits...
At age 62, your payment would be about...$ 940 a month
If you continue working until...
your full retirement age (67 years), your payment would be about ....$ 1,363 a month
age 70, your payment would be about ....$ 1,699 a month

▼ ***Disability**   You have earned enough credits to qualify for benefits. If you became disabled right now,
Your payment would be about...$ 1,248 a month

▼ ***Family**   If you get retirement or disability benefits, your spouse and children also may qualify for benefits.

▼ ***Survivors**   You have earned enough credits for your family to receive survivors benefits. If you die this year, certain members of your family **may** qualify for the following benefits.

Your child..$ 972 a month
Your spouse who is caring for your child..$ 972 a month
Your spouse, if benefits start at full retirement age ....$ 1,297 a month
Total family benefits cannot be more than ....$ 2,386 a month

Your spouse or minor child may be eligible for a special one-time death benefit of $255.

▼ **Medicare**   You have enough credits to qualify for Medicare at age 65. Even if you do not retire at age 65, be sure to contact Social Security three months before your 65th birthday to enroll in Medicare.

*Your estimated benefits are based on current law. Congress has made changes to the law in the past and can do so at any time. The law governing benefit amounts may change because, by 2041, the payroll taxes collected will be enough to pay only about 74 percent of scheduled benefits.

We based your benefit estimates on these facts:
Your date of birth .... May 5, 1965
Your estimated taxable earnings per year after 2005 .... $37,276
Your Social Security number (only the last four digits
are shown to help prevent identity theft) XXX-XX-1234

2

benefits. I guess that makes up for the people who die the day they receive their first Social Security check.

I am a firm believer in asset allocation in your investments. That means your investments are properly diversified into different categories according to *your* risk profile, *your* behavior towards investing, and *your* goals. If you are still young, you might be a moderately aggressive type of investor. In that case, your portfolio might look like this:

>   Stock, also called equity mutual funds – 80-85%
>   Bonds, sometimes called fixed mutual funds – 15-20%

This means every investment will be in this structure. For example, your retirement plan at work would be invested 80% in stock mutual funds such as: growth, growth and income, value, and international. 20% would be in bond mutual funds such as: short-term, intermediate and hi-yield. Your IRA would have the same diversification but in a different mutual fund family. Any Variable Universal Life (VUL) insurance polices would have the same per-cents. As you get older or your risk profile changes for any reason, these percents change as well.

The broad categories and possible allocations as an investor are as follows, with the stock percentage first then the bond percentage.

Aggressive	Moderately Aggressive	Moderate	Moderately Conservative	Conservative
95% / 5%	80% / 20%	70% / 30%	60% / 40%	50% / 50%

The graph on the next page (142) shows a hypothetical moderate portfolio.

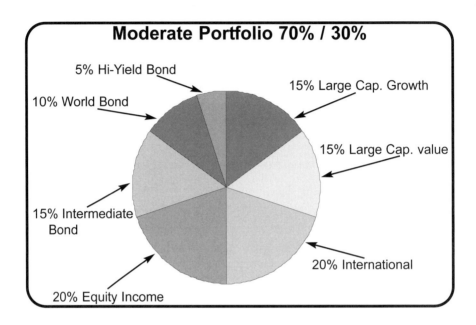

If you like to invest in individual stocks and not mutual funds make sure you are in a couple of different industries – and you do not need more than 12 different stocks at a time. I can hear the wire-house stockbrokers cursing me as I write this.

I *am* a stockbroker *and* a registered investment advisor. I am personally more comfortable letting the mutual fund managers (who are smarter than I'll ever be, have more resources and research available than I'll ever have, and have access to more staff than I can dream of) make the individual stock moves for me in my mutual funds. I like to say that mutual funds are more forgiving than individual stocks. Granted, it is not as sexy as owning individual stocks, but I've learned the hard way that slow and consistent wins the race.

Another reason that mutual funds are good investments is their diversity. Remember the saying, "Don't put all your eggs in one basket?" That is the idea behind diversification. The money is invested in hundreds of companies, which reduces volatility. So if there is one bad investment, it will typically be offset by the better results in the rest of the portfolio.

Since there are so many companies in the portfolio, you don't have to worry about having *Enron* or *WorldCom* in the mix. Each company represents such a small percentage of the fund that if one goes bankrupt, it doesn't hurt the whole mutual fund. Would you rather own one store or the whole mall? Mutual funds are a great way to invest internationally and take advantage of some incredible companies overseas as well.

Mutual funds are also very liquid because you can sell at any time to get cash quickly. You can have withdrawals automatically deducted from your mutual fund account and deposited in your bank account if you wish, and vice versa.

Also, if you are investing in bond mutual funds, a nice benefit is that you can receive a monthly income from the dividends, instead of waiting every six months for the dividend from an individual bond.

I believe mutual funds offer several advantages over individual stocks and individual bonds. This is including the often overlooked aspect that it is usually less expensive to own mutual funds than stocks.

There are two large categories of mutual funds, they are called either *load* or *no-load*. Load means there is a sales charge, which is how the advisor and broker/dealer get paid, each getting a percent of the sales charge. No-load means no sales charge and no advisor. You can do your mutual fund investing yourself by using the internet and the mutual fund company's 800 number. Since there is no advisor, there is no sales charge by the mutual fund company. All this means it can be inexpensive owning mutual funds if you decide to do your investing yourself.

If, however, you are not comfortable investing by yourself and want the services of a financial advisor, you need to know about mutual fund share classes and the costs associated with each.

Class A shares have an *up-front* sales charge or load that is taken off your initial investment. All mutual funds have operating expenses and Class A shares usually have lower expenses than other share classes.

Class B shares have a *deferred* sales charge. This is a sales charge or load that investors pay when selling shares during a five to ten year holding period from the time of initial investment. Class B shares have the highest annual operating expenses of the share classes; however, at the end of the holding period, these funds automatically convert to A shares

Class C shares do not have up-front or deferred sales charge, they do have an annual level-load that is typically 1% every year. Their operating expenses are lower than B shares but higher than A shares. All three share classes have pros and cons and that is why it is so important to know the purpose of your investments.

Knowing what your financial goals are, and what you are trying to accomplish with your investing, is just as important as where you put your money. Also, now understanding your motive behind your investments, to be able to give more to the less fortunate, should be enough reason for you to accumulate as much as you can and make sure your investments are doing the best they can. Our good stewardship will always glorify Jesus. As with all things, cast your cares upon the Lord and pray for His direction and leading.

James 1:5 *If any of you lacks wisdom, let him ask of God, who gives to all liberally and without reproach, and it will be given to him.*

Risk Tolerance Questionaire

Please answer the following questions by circling the number opposite the answer that best describes your opinion. Add up the circled numbers to determine your score. Your total score will indicate your risk profile.

1. **Protecting the principal of my investment is more important than achieving significant growth.**
   * ✱ Strongly Agree 0
   * ✱ Agree 4
   * ✱ Disagree 11
   * ✱ Strongly Disagree 16

2. **Which of the following investment strategies do you prefer?**
   * ✱ One that seeks to avoid loss. 0
   * ✱ One that has the potential for both moderate gain and moderate loss? 9
   * ✱ One that maximizes potential gain regardless of the potential for loss. 18

3. **Assuming you own a stock fund that has lost 15% of its value over the past year, despite solid performance in previous years, and that this year's loss is consistent with the performance of similar funds during the past year, would you:**
   * ✱ Sell all of your fund shares? 0
   * ✱ Sell some, but not all your fund shares? 4
   * ✱ Hold all your fund shares? 9
   * ✱ Increase your investment in the fund by buying more shares? 12

4. **Inflation can greatly reduce the real rate of return on your investment over time. Which of the following are you willing to accept:**
   * ✱ Minimal potential for loss, although investment may only keep pace with inflation. 0
   * ✱ Moderate potential for loss and lower volatility in trying to exceed the rate of inflation. . . 9
   * ✱ Significant potential for loss and high volatility in trying to greatly exceed the rate of inflation 18

5. **Which of the following hypothetical investment portfolio returns, over a one-year period, do you prefer?**
   * ✱ A likely return of 6% and slight chance of losing value. 0
   * ✱ A likely return of 10% and moderate chance of losing value. 9
   * ✱ A likely return of 14% and significant chance of losing value. 18

6. **Which of the following hypothetical portfolio average annual returns, over a three-year period, do you prefer?**
   * ✱ 0% to 10% 0
   * ✱ -5% to 18% 9
   * ✱ -10% to 26% 18

TOTAL SCORE:

If you scored
0 - 26 Wanting greater stability and a lower risk – you are **conservative**.
27 - 48 Looking to strike a balance between safety and growth, but are concerned with preserving your existing accumulation – you are **moderately conservative**.
49 - 70 Looking to strike a balance between safety and growth, but are willing to take somewhat more risk to achieve greater growth potential – you are **moderately agressive**.
71 -100 Comfortable with a higher level of risk – you are **aggressive**.

Chapter 8 – Accumulation
Review Points

- God wants us to earn as much as we can and to accumulate as much as possible for the purpose of giving it away.

- God's Perfect Economic Plan is that there would be equality among people.

- The Lord gives to us according to our abilities.

- Asking these questions will determine where and how to invest:
  - ◈ What is the purpose of this investment?
  - ◈ When do I need the money?
  - ◈ What is my risk tolerance?
  - ◈ How will taxes and inflation affect this investment?
  - ◈ How much can I invest?

- Portfolio diversification and rebalancing are the important ingredients of the recipe for successful investing.

- The rule of thumb for retirement income is that 75% - 80% of present income would create a similar lifestyle after retirement (adjusted for inflation).

Preservation

Luke 12:42-44

And the Lord said, "Who then is that faithful and wise steward, whom his master will make ruler over his household, to give them their portion of food in due season? Blessed is that servant whom his master will find so doing when he comes. Truly, I say to you that he will make him ruler over all that he has.

The third and final segment of the Lord's Financial Plan is the most intimidating. Because of this, most people put it off, or even worse, never do it. It is the final act of financial stewardship. It is called *preservation* or estate planning.

Preservation is the accumulation of all your labors and God's blessings to you and your family and what you are going to do with them after you are no longer alive. In other words, the *distribution* of everything God has entrusted you with. The idea of being able to leave a legacy should be our incentive, and glorifying God our purpose. In this chapter we will discuss what the Bible says about the preservation process, the tools available, and the cost of *not* planning for the distribution of your estate.

Some people think estate planning is only for the rich, but almost every adult needs some sort of an estate plan. Estate planning provides you with the peace of mind of knowing your assets are going *where* you want, to *whom* you want, and *when* you want. The *why* being that we are accountable to God Almighty.

Romans 14:12 says each of us will give an account of himself to God. Paul was talking to and about Christians in this verse of the letter he wrote to the Roman church. Preserving our estate and estate planning is our responsibility. It should not be taken lightly and adequate time should be spent on it.

Let's read what the wisest man who ever lived, Solomon, says about our final act of stewardship in Ecclesiastes 5:10-6:6. It is a long section, but to get a good understanding of what God is trying to tell us, we must include every verse.

He who loves silver will not be satisfied with silver; Nor he who loves abundance, with increase. This also is vanity. When goods increase, they increase who eat them; So what profit have the owners except to see them with their eyes? The sleep of a laboring man is sweet, whether he eats little or much; but the abundance of the rich will not permit him to sleep.

There is a severe evil which I have seen under the sun: Riches kept for their owner to his hurt. But those riches perish through misfortune; when he begets a son, there is nothing in his hand. As he came from his mother's womb, naked shall he return, to go as he came; And he shall take nothing from his labor which he may carry away in his hand.

And this also is a severe evil – just exactly as he came, so shall he go. And what profit has he who has labored for the wind? All his days he also eats in darkness, and he has much sorrow and sickness and anger.

Here is what I have seen: It is good and fitting for one to eat and drink, and to enjoy the good of all his labor in which he toils under the sun all the days of his life which God gives him; for it is his heritage. As for every man to whom God has given riches and wealth, and given him the power to eat of it, to receive his heritage and rejoice in his labor – this is the gift of God. For he will not dwell unduly on the days of his life, because God keeps him busy with the joy of his heart.

Ch. 6:1 There is an evil which I have seen under the sun, and it is common among men: A man to whom God has given riches and wealth and honor, so that he lacks nothing for himself of all he desires; yet God does not give him power to eat of it, but a foreigner consumes it. This is vanity, and it is an evil affliction.

If a man begets a hundred children and lives many years, so that the days of his years are many, but his soul is not satisfied with goodness, or indeed he has no burial, I say that a stillborn child is better than he – for it comes in vanity and departs in darkness, and its name is covered with darkness. Though it has not seen the sun or known anything, this has more rest than that man, even if he lives a thousand years twice – but has not seen goodness. Do not all go to one place?

Solomon says the more we make, the more we spend. Even 3000 years ago this was a problem. Because of the anxiety this causes, the rich man cannot rest, while the laborer does not allow this to bother him as much and he sleeps without the same worries of the very rich, who have much more to be concerned about, especially taxes.

Under today's tax law, some beneficiaries of an estate have to pay probate costs, death tax, and estate tax which are due nine months after the surviving parent's death. Estate taxes is for people who have a net worth or "estate" of $2 million or more.

Two million dollars is the current estate tax exemption dollar amount, or the amount that is "exempt" from estate taxes. This estate tax exemption amount is going up almost every year and is scheduled to go back *down* to $1 million in 2011, with no estate tax in 2010. This is yet another good reason to know your net worth.

Solomon calls it a *severe evil* to not leave anything to his children and to have his riches perish through misfortune, or literally, bad business.

The misfortune, or bad business of riches perishing that Solomon speaks of, could be avoided with an estate plan that includes properly set-up trusts and wills (which will be explained later in the chapter). An estate plan that will preserve and distribute almost all of your assets in a timely and efficient manner to the people and places you want it to go, without your beneficiaries paying additional taxes.

Another severe evil Solomon mentions is eating in darkness and having much sorrow, sickness, and anger. If this type of catastrophe occurs, such as a paralyzing accident, coma, or even dementia, then having a Durable Power of Attorney for Healthcare, or DPOAHC, will help your family.

A Durable Power of Attorney for Healthcare, also known as "Advanced Health Directive" or a "Living Will" depending on the state you live in, allows you to appoint someone, your agent, to make medical decisions for you on your behalf in case you are too ill or are unable to make them. While you have a sound mind and the ability to think clearly is the time to appoint someone, because you obviously cannot do this if you are in a coma. It is usually your spouse and vise-versa; however, you still need a secondary or contingent agent in case both are incapable of making the decisions.

Without a Durable Power of Attorney for Healthcare, the courts will appoint someone on your behalf to make the medical decisions you may or may not have wanted. Even the spouse and children are powerless, as we saw in the Terri Schiavo case a few years ago.

The Durable Power of Attorney for Healthcare does the following:

* ✴ Decides ahead of time what medical procedures you do or do not want.

* Assists your family in making very difficult decisions.
* Makes sure *your* wishes are followed even if they are different from your family's wishes.

Another problem of not having a Durable Power of Attorney for Healthcare, in case of a medical situation, is the time delay of the courts appointing someone, which can take days. Or, you can have a DPOAHC and the person *you* choose making the decisions *you* originally wanted immediately.

There is also a cost involved for the courts to appoint someone, called a conservator. These costs are eliminated with a DPOAHC. Can you see now why Solomon called this a severe evil? You and your family lose control and it could have been avoided. If you are an adult, this type of planning should be done.

Solomon says having much sorrow is a severe evil. Could he be talking about the distress and regret of poverty? Long-term care costs can be devastating to the net worth, which is the number one decimation of an estate today. We are living longer and dying more slowly. Every day 237 people turn 100 years old. The costs of long term care have skyrocketed and the inflation rate for medical services is close to 6% per year.

The monthly rate of $4,000 – $9,000 and the average stay of two and a half years in a nursing home can wipe out a large percent of an estate. These costs are not including the time *prior* to going into a nursing home, where people are doing everything they can to keep their loved ones at home with help from aides, nurses, and home modifications.

For those who have substantial assets and can afford a monthly premium of $250 - $500 for a couple, long-term care insurance is something they must consider, especially if they want to leave as much as they can to their beneficiaries and charities.

To be blessed by God with riches and wealth is a gift from God. We are to enjoy it, share it, and then distribute it – to pass it on. Solomon says it is evil, and even common, for man to have a foreigner consume the riches and wealth. Why give all this to the government, courts, and hospitals when it can be avoided? Even a still-born child, or a miscarriage, is better than a man that does not leave an inheritance. *"What profit has he who labored for the wind?"*

The Lord tells us the days of our lives will have meaning and purpose if we allow ourselves to enjoy what God has given us. And then the Lord gives one of the best promises in all of Scripture at the end of chapter five:

> *For he will not dwell unduly on the days of his life, because God keeps him busy with the joy of his heart.*

How exciting this life can be when we do what the Lord asks us to do. To eat, drink, and be merry, and the Lord will fill our lives with a supernatural joy that can only come from our Father in Heaven.

Knowing that God honors the *preservation* of what He has entrusted to us, and knowing what He doesn't want to happen, we see that our role as stewards never ends. Now we have to create a strategy for our estate.

1.) *Who* receives it?
2.) *When* do they receive it?
3.) *What* do they receive?

Who receives your assets when you die? Traditionally, this has always been to our children. I want you to prayerfully consider how much you want to leave to your children. I talked earlier in the protection chapter about leaving 10% to your home church as a beneficiary in your life insurance. Does this mean you leave the balance of your assets to your children? I am not so sure.

There are a few questions you must think about first. Are your children walking with the Lord? Have they been unproductive waiting for their inheritance? Or, have they proven to be good stewards?

> Ecc. 2:20, 21 *Therefore I turned my heart and despaired of all the labor in which I had toiled under the sun. For there is a man whose labor is with wisdom, knowledge, and skill; Yet he must leave his heritage to a man who has not labored for it. This also is vanity and a great evil.*

We know the Prodigal Son wasted half of his father's estate. None of that money went to do the Lord's work, just the opposite in fact. We can sometimes spoil our children by leaving them too much and not allowing them to appreciate hard work, perseverance, and discipline.

One of my main purposes in writing this book is for people to realize how important it is to give to God and His work. It is God's Perfect Economic Plan – that there be an equality. We cannot out-give God. The more we give, the more joy we receive. It should not be a contest or a race to see who *has* the most, but who can *give* the most.

It is all relative. For example, if your net worth is $10,000 and you give $5000 for God's Kingdom when you pass away, you have given 50% of your estate. Can you imagine how effective God's Church would be if all believers gave half of their assets to Christian ministries? I sincerely believe you should consider leaving a large portion of your estate for charitable planning.

Unfortunately, most Christians do not feel the same way as I do. As we enter in the age of the greatest wealth transfer in the history of mankind, most people want to leave it all to their children. I have heard too many times, "This is for my kids and they can do what they want with it," or "My kids will tithe when they get it," or "I gave enough when I was alive." I wonder if God thinks they gave back enough to Him?

There are several tools available, which we will go over, and many potential financial benefits of charitable giving, for example:

* It will provide an income tax deduction.
* In many cases, it can avoid payment of capital gains tax.
* May *increase* your personal after-tax cash flow.
* May *increase* the amount passing to your heirs.

The charitable planning tools are many for those with sizable assets. But there are ways for the "average" folks to give, also. The most common is to make a donation with cash or with a check. The IRS allows a write-off or deduction from your income taxes on your donations up to 50% of your adjusted gross income.

Some people however, just do not have the extra cash to give. I think of older people who really want to give who are living off Social Security and a small pension. However, they might have some stock that they have owned for several years, but do not want to sell the stock because they would owe capital gains tax after the sale. It would be better to give or tithe these stocks than it is to give cash.

When they donate the stocks, they avoid any capital gains tax and the non-profit church that receives the stock does not pay taxes, either. The donor would still receive the write-off on the full amount of the gift from the IRS. In this case, this older couple could give stock for their tithing, receive a tax deduction, avoid any capital gains tax, and the church gets a donation that they would normally not receive.

Many people think they have to sell their shares first and then give cash to their favorite charity, then pay the taxes later. Only do this if the share price is *below* what you purchased it for. This way you can deduct or write off the *loss* on the stock *and* get a deduction for the donation. But if the stock has gone up, then give the stock or mutual fund *directly* to the ministry. Unfortunately, a large percentage of churches do not know what I just wrote about and do not have a stock brokerage account open for people to give stock or mutual funds.

It has become my ministry and passion to help churches increase their giving receipts. Most churches are understaffed and overworked. They need additional income to support more paid employees to help the pastors implement life-changing programs. Churches need income to nurture short-term and long-term missionaries so more people can go out and spread the Gospel.

If the churches are not going to take advantage of all the tools available, then other secular non-profits will, and the church will not get anything after "feeding" their flock for a lifetime. Unfortunately, this happens every day.

There are more fancy ways to give for the wealthy people, which may not apply to you, but I think it is important to know what is available.

The *Charitable Remainder Trust* (CRT) is one of the most popular gifting strategies because of the tax benefits and the income it provides to the donor. A CRT works very well with assets that have appreciated a lot, like property or an investment that was purchased a long time ago that has really gone up in value.

The reason it works so well is that these assets have a capital gains tax liability. When these appreciable assets are put in a CRT, neither the donor nor the charity, which will eventually receive the gift, has to pay any long-term capital gains tax.

For example, you have an investment you bought for $100,000 and many years later it is now worth $300,000. If you sold this asset and gave cash, you would get the charitable gift deduction for income tax purposes, but would still owe capital gains tax. However, if you gave it to your CRT with charities as the beneficiaries, you would get credit for gifting the whole amount of $300,000 for tax purposes and the charities eventually get to use,

Charitable Remainder Trust
CRT

The donor transfers an asset to the trustee of the charitable remainder trust (CRT) and receives a fixed dollar amount for each year thereafter. A current income tax deduction is also available.

When the donor or other named beneficiary dies, the remaining trust assets pass to the designated charity.

Donor

* Transfers asset to CRT.

* Receives dollar amount each year.

* Receives income tax deduction.

Asset

Annual Annuity Payout

Income Tax Deduction

CRT

* Trustee sells asset and reinvests for greater return.

* Pays no capital gains tax on the appreciation at the time of sale.

* Trustee pays dollar amount yearly.

Charitable Organization

* Receives any assets remaining in the trust when the beneficiary is deceased..

After the beneficiary is deceased the remaining trust assets pass to the charity.

when the second spouse dies, potentially, the whole $300,000. Plus, you get a new income stream for at least 20 years. The income might not have been an option prior to the CRT, because the investment asset did not provide any income. It's a win-win-win situation.

More specifically, the donor transfers some type of asset to *his* Charitable Remainder Trust that he had created under the laws of his state. The donor then specifies how he wants the income paid to him after the CRT *sells* the asset. The asset is sold and then the cash is invested, thereby creating an income stream. This income to the donor could be a fixed amount or a variable amount for a life-time, any period of time up to 20 years, or a period of years for chil-dren to receive the income. At the end of this income period, what-ever amount of the investment is left then becomes the property of the charity, and because of the incredible law of compounding interest, this amount is usually higher than the original gift.

Because assets transferred to the CRT by the donor will be used for charitable purposes in the future, the donor is allowed income tax, gift tax, and estate tax deductions in the year of the gift and possibly up to five years thereafter. The donor can also change the beneficiaries of the CRT at any time, as long as it still goes to a non-profit organization. [See chart on the left.]

A *Charitable Gift Annuity* (CGA) is another wonderful way of helping a charity, *and* creates an income stream to the donor *and* reduces the income tax, estate, and capital gains tax situation. Similar to a CRT except the donor gives the asset direct to the char-ity irrevocably (cannot change it), not to a trust, and the charity then makes an unsecured promise to pay an income stream to the donor or someone else the donor designates, through an annuity. This is less expensive than a CRT, in fact, it does not cost the donor any-thing and you can give almost any amount or asset. [See chart on next page.]

Charitable Gift Annuity
CGA

The donor transfers an asset to a charity and receives a fixed dollar amount, set at the time the gift is made, each year thereafter. A current income tax deduction is also available.

When the donor or other named beneficiary dies, the charity has no furthur financial obligations to pay.

Donor

Asset ➡

* Transfers asset to charity.

* Receives annual payout.

Annual Annuity ⬅

* Receives income tax deduction.

Income Tax Deduction ⬅

CGA

* Charity sells asset and reinvests for greater return.

* Charity pays no capital gains tax on the appreciation at the time of sale.

* Charity pays a fixed dollar amount, established at time of gift each year for lifetime of beneficiary.

After the beneficiary is deceased the charity has no further obligations to pay.

There are also many other ways including *Charitable Remainder Annuity Trust* (CRAT), *Charitable Remainder Unitrust* (CRUT), even a *Flip CRUT.* These examples are usually for the purpose of lowering your estate tax liability and at the same time being able to give as much as possible to the non-profit organization of your choice and creating an income stream for you and your spouse for several years. You can give any amount; however, these examples are usually for people with large estates. But every gift counts in the Lord's accounting book, not just the rich. Remember the widow that Jesus talks about at the temple. She was only able to give two mites and He said she put in more than all.

> Luke 21:1-4 *And He (Jesus) looked up and saw the rich putting their gifts into the treasury, and He saw also a certain poor widow putting in two mites, so He said, "Truly I say to you that this poor widow has put in more than all; for all these out of their abundance have put in offerings for God, but she out of her poverty put in all the livelihood that she had."*

We just talked about some of the ways to answer "Who receives it?" This is the first question to ask in developing an estate plan strategy. What percent do you want to give to your children, church, or favorite charity? Or, what percent do you want to give to another non-profit organization – the IRS, for *not* planning your estate?

Now we ask the second question, "When do they receive it?" If you, your attorney, and financial advisor have properly prepared your estate plan, everything could be distributed within 60 days. The assets will go into different trusts upon the death of the first spouse (depending on the size of the estate) and then the assets will be distributed *after* the death of the second spouse, according to the directions of the will and the beneficiary designations.

I recommend the portion you are leaving to your children be given at different ages in their lives. For example, 25% given at age 21, 25% given at age 25, 25% given at 30 years old, and 25% at 40 years old. The reason for this is the reality of a possible divorce, bad business deal, or some other catastrophe.

We can go back to the Prodigal Son again. He was too young

and immature for the sudden wealth he received. Look at all the destroyed lives in the sports and entertainment fields. It is too much, too soon, for too many. Another possible method to distribute the estate is according to your values and principals such as an "education" approach. One-third given if they get a Bachelor's degree, another third if they get a Master's and the balance given if they get a Doctorate. There are endless ways to be creative; but it is just as important to pass on your values as well as your money.

Lastly, "What do they receive?"

It is the little things that can cause conflict. It is not always the house people want, but the personal items left behind. Because the Bible, wallet, watch, or a collection say more about the deceased, these can be very valuable to the children and grandchildren. Talk to your family about these types of items and ask them who wants what when everyone is together.

The same is true regarding any real estate owned. Discuss with the beneficiaries what they want to do with your home. Do they want to sell it? Rent it out? Or does someone want to move in?

Being open and honest early is the best way to avoid problems later. I recommend that families make a specific time to discuss all these details. Let the family know you are getting all your affairs in order and need to discuss this unpleasant but necessary topic of someday not being here.

Children with older parents can honor their father and mother by helping them through this planning process. Set some time with them to discuss the benefits of proper planning and the final act of stewardship.

The preservation section, the final part of the Lord's Financial Plan, links to one of the first items discussed, and that is the importance of knowing your net worth. Here is a good example why. I know a couple who were both 70 years old. They had served the Lord their entire lives as professors and teachers in a variety of dis-

tinguished schools.

Since they had retired, the husband served on several Christian ministry boards, he was planting a church, and was the president of a school for pastors (you never really retire from service to the Lord). After they did a net worth statement, they realized they had a large estate.

They were so busy serving the Lord they did not realize how many different accounts they both had and how much they had been blessed by God. They were worth millions and their family would have had to pay millions for their estate tax. Since that time they have implemented some strategies discussed in this chapter and now they are able to give to family, churches, and ministries almost the entire estate instead of losing a large portion to taxes. It all started with figuring out their net worth.

Now that the strategy is created – the who, when, and what – it is time to understand the tools that are available. The basic will, or pour over will, is the most common estate planning tool and an essential part. It is the primary legal document for transferring your assets upon death. It is a document drafted by an attorney during your lifetime, which does many things. The basic will determines:

1.) Where to distribute all your possessions
2.) Names an executor of your estate
3.) Says who you want as guardian of your minor children
4.) Gives instructions to any trusts that have been set up.

Choosing a legal guardian for your children is one of the toughest decisions you will ever have to make. But if you don't make a decision, the courts will make it for you. A few thoughts on this might help you narrow down your options.

* People who have not raised children do not usually make good guardians.

* The people you choose should be Christians like you, so
  your children will continue to grow spiritually.
* Of course, you need to be sure they will accept this great
  responsibility.

If you die intestate, or without a will, state law determines
where your property goes and who watches your children as legal
guardians. This is why I say that almost every adult needs some
sort of estate plan and almost 70% do *not* have one according to

---

Every adult needs some sort of estate plan.

---

recent studies. Having a basic will drawn up by an established
estate planning attorney can be done for about $100. It is worth the
time and money. Your children are obviously your greatest treas-
ures, gifts from God, and as an act of stewardship of parenting, you
need a will!

The executor of the estate has several important responsibilities:

1. Administering the estate and distributing the assets
   according to the will.
2. Making tax decisions with the assistance of a CPA by filing tax returns, paying any federal, state, or estate taxes,
   and receiving the required minimum distributions
   (RMD) from the IRAs, if that applies.
3. Paying all the bills that are owed.
4. Making sure the beneficiaries have received all the proper payouts on the life insurance policies, retirement
   plans, and annuities.

Your basic will also gives specific instructions for the trusts that
have been created if you own real estate, investments, bank

accounts, or a business or businesses. We will discuss trusts next. I wanted you to understand first what the will does and its importance. What we just talked about is a basic will or pour-over will.

The Durable Power of Attorney for Healthcare mentioned earlier is a separate legal document that should accompany your wills. Put them in a binder in a safe place and give a copy to your executor/trustee, and even your medical doctor could have a copy.

A Revocable Living Trust is a legal document created by an attorney that works in conjunction with a will. It provides direction for the management and distribution of your assets upon your death. After the trust has been created, you place assets into the trust by changing the title from your name to the trust name.

For example, your home might now be titled as John Smith and Ann Smith, joint owners. The new title will be the Smith Family Trust. The trust will also provide instructions for the management of this property and other assets that have been placed in the trust.

Probate is the process of proving and administering a will under court supervision.

Having a Revocable Living Trust allows you to avoid probate. But, what in the world is probate? Probate is the process of proving and administering a will under the supervision of the courts.

The cost of probate varies from state to state, but the average charge is 3%-5% of your total estate. The courts have to assign a probate attorney to your case who must verify all the documents and figure out who gets what and when. This attorney must be paid and that is why the costs of probate are high. It can take a lot of time, especially if there are several family members.

One extreme example of what *not* having proper wills and trusts can do to the family is the case of Jerry Garcia of the rock band *The Grateful Dead*. Jerry Garcia died in 1995 and ex-wives, children, partners, and lenders are still contesting his estate. We know this because his estate is a matter of public record and any privacy he may have wanted is eliminated. Probate costs money, takes time, and makes your estate public – it could have been avoided with a trust.

Even during Jesus' days there were disputes about inheritances. The people at that time went to the religious leaders to settle the conflicts. Jesus stayed out of the argument and then issued a warning.

> Luke 12:13-15 *Then one from the crowd said to Him, "Teacher, tell my brother to divide the inheritance with me." But Jesus said to him, "Man, who made me a judge or arbitrator over you?" And He said to them, "Take heed and beware of covetousness, for one's life does not consist in the abundance of the things he possesses."*

Some assets do not go through probate regardless of whether you have a will or not. An easy way to remember what does not go through probate and remains out of your trust is anything that has a beneficiary attached to it, such as life insurance, annuities, retirement plans like 401(k) or 403(b), and IRAs. The reason is that you have already decided who is going to get the money when you die and this does not have to be proved by the courts, because it was established when you originally opened these accounts in the beneficiary section of the application. However, you can change beneficiaries at any time.

Real estate, businesses, savings, checking accounts, and investments do not have beneficiaries assigned to them and will go to probate unless properly avoided by renaming these assets in the trust name. This is why it is extremely important to know and update your beneficiaries. Divorces, births, adoptions, deaths, and remarriages happen, so the beneficiaries must change, also.

The estate tax structure is always changing and it is one of the favorite targets politically. If you own substantial assets, you need to have a professional planner determine if you have an estate tax liability. If you are married, then at your death everything goes to your spouse. When the remaining spouse dies is when the estate taxes are due and they are to be paid to the IRS within nine months.

To pay the tax, the beneficiaries can liquidate or sell some assets to pay the taxes, but it might take longer than nine months to sell. They might get less because it is a "quick" sale, or it could possibly be a down market at that time. To pay the estate tax, people can borrow from the IRS to pay off the amount due; however, I cannot think of an uglier option.

The best way to pay the estimated estate taxes is to have an insurance policy in place, called second-to-die life insurance, on the amount of money that is estimated to be due. The second-to-die life insurance is one policy for two lives. Nothing is paid out until the second spouse dies. The problems with this strategy are that someone may be uninsurable at their age because of health problems, and it can be an expensive policy that needs to be paid every year. However, the cost is always less than the benefit received.

Earlier in the protection section I said the need for life insurance fluctuates in a person's lifetime. The need goes up again if you have an estate tax problem. The beneficiary gets the death benefit of the life insurance quickly and usually free from any taxes and is able to pay the estate taxes, and most importantly, the children, church, and charities get the whole amount of the estate!

I must be careful of over-simplifying using life insurance to pay estate taxes. To do this correctly and depending on the size of the potential estate tax liability, an *Irrevocable Life Insurance Trust* (ILIT) should be created. This way, using a second-to-die life insurance policy, with the ILIT named as the owner of the policy, will keep the death benefit *out* of the estate.

If the life insurance did not go into the ILIT it would add even *more* estate tax liability to the family because the life insurance death benefit would increase the estate. But when done correctly, and when the second spouse dies, the ILIT receives the death benefit tax-free. The beneficiaries of the ILIT can then pay all the taxes that are due in a timely manner and they would not have to liquidate any assets if they did not want to.

Remember that preserving your estate is not a one-time process, and it can take several months to get everything in its proper place. Not everyone will have the opportunity that Jacob had in the second to last chapter in Genesis, where he gave instructions to his sons and "breathed his last."

Even after the estate planning is completed, it should be reviewed at least every other year, because of the potential changes in family structure, asset changes, and all the tax code changes. I suggest doing this around your wedding anniversary to demonstrate your love to your spouse, or maybe a child's birth date. Just make sure it gets done and with the help of a qualified financial planner and estate-planning attorney.

> Psalm 49:10 *For he sees wise men die; Likewise the fool and the senseless person perish, and leave their wealth to others.*

This is the basic estate plan for people who own a home or property. It will consist of the following, which we have already discussed and which can be done at the same time are:

1. Wills for husband and wife
2. Revocable Family Living Trust
3. Powers of Attorney for husband
4. Powers of Attorney for wife

For families that God has blessed who have assets over $2 million should consult with a qualified financial planner and estate planning attorney to see what strategies should be implemented.

The strategies explained so far would help more than 95% of the people in America. The ultra high net-worth people need sophisticated strategies that will not be explained in this book.

There are several ways to reduce your estate tax liability. If your networth is in the millions (this is easier than we think when we consider housing prices) then think about *charitable remainder trusts* and *charitable gift annuities* to lower your estate, which in turn lowers your estate tax. One does not *have* to be a multi-millionaire to use these tools though, they are available to everyone. They are just a couple of ways to give and lower estate taxes.

You can also give to each family member up to $12,000 every year (this anount changes from year to year) without paying a gift tax, and the receiving family members do not pay any tax on the gift. For example, if you have five grandchildren, you can give each one a gift of $12,000 and put it towards their college savings. You reduce your estate by $60,000 and have also jumpstarted the grandkid's college education. In Acts 21:35 Paul is quoting Jesus when he says it is better to give than receive and we can see this holding true especially in the area of preserving our estate.

A lot of people consider their grandchildren in their giving or gifting strategy. An excellent way is to open a college account, called a 529 Plan, on behalf of the grandchildren. Because of the flexibility, the giving limits, and the tax deferred growth of the mutual funds in the 529 Plan, they make remarkable gifts. Just remember, it is a mutual fund investment and there is not a guarantee on the growth, they can go down in value

Another benefit is if the grandparent remains the owner of the 529 Plan and the grandchild is the beneficiary, the amount invested stays out of the parent's estate. This will help the parents qualify for more financial aid at college time. I believe the College 529 Plan has been one of the best investments that has been created and could be considered in your giving strategy.

I've talked a lot about life insurance and what it can do. One more thought about it before we finish this chapter. A powerful way to leave a legacy is by giving the gift of a life insurance policy to your church. You can have the ability of making a substantially larger gift and leaving a tremendous legacy, *and* your family still receives your assets.

One way is to make your church the primary beneficiary and you make the premium payments. Another way is to purchase a life insurance policy on yourself and make the church both the policy owner and the beneficiary. Include in your contributions to the church an amount equal to the monthly payments. The church then makes the premium payments for the life insurance policy. This can be tricky because of the bookkeeping and the commitment by the donor, but if the life insurance was a cash value policy and the donor stops making the contributions, the church receives the cash value in the policy. I must mention that these types of gifts are an offering and not tithing. This is over and above your normal tithing amount, which is based on your gross income.

> 2 Chronicles 31:10, *And Azariah the chief priest, from the house of Zadok, answered him (King Hezekiah) and said, "Since the people began to bring the offerings into the house of the LORD, we have had enough to eat, and have plenty left, for the LORD has blessed his people; and what is left is this great abundance."*

Earlier, I talked about giving so we can be more like God who is the ultimate giver. We can't take our money with us but we can sure send it on ahead.

> Luke 12: 33, 34 Jesus talking to the multitudes says: *Sell what you have and give alms; provide for yourselves money bags which do not grow old, a treasure in the Heavens that does not fail, where no thief approaches nor moth destroys. For where your treasure is, there your heart will be also."*

Chapter 9 – Preservation
Review Points

- Preservation or estate planning is our final act of stewardship.

- If you have a child, own a home, or are married you will need some form of estate planning.

- Create a strategy for your estate by answering these three questions:
  - ✧ Who receives it?
  - ✧ When do they receive it?
  - ✧ What do they receive?

- Charitable gifting should be part of our estate planning and four popular ways are:
  - ✧ Giving stocks and mutual funds directly to church or ministry
  - ✧ Charitable Remainder Trust
  - ✧ Charitable Gift Annuity
  - ✧ Beneficiary of life insurance and retirement plans

- Necessary items of a typical estate plan for a married couple who own a home:
  - ✧ Will
    - ✧ Names executor of estate.
    - ✧ Names legal guardian of minor children.
    - ✧ Gives instructions for the trusts.
  - ✧ Family Living Trust – avoids probate and keeps things private.
  - ✧ Durable Power of Attorney for Healthcare – appoints someone to make medical decisions on your behalf.

Alexa R. Singleton

Gaining financial freedom in accordance with The Lord's Financial plan is a joyous accomplishment!

Conclusion

Proverbs 16:16

How much better to get wisdom than gold! And to get understanding is to be chosen rather than silver.

Ninety-five percent of all people, by the time they reach the age of 65 are either dead or dead broke. Why is that? We obviously don't know the answer to the dead part other than it is God's Will. But why are only 5% of the people financially independent?

I wondered why this was for a long time and I have found the answer. The people who are financially secure *are the ones who would rather earn interest than pay interest.* They live within their incomes and do not go in debt. It has become a habit for them and because of this, they have money to invest.

This 5% group of people may or may not be the most astute investors, but they know the value of compounding interest. They are also patient and are willing to wait some time before purchasing expensive items and they want to pay in cash.

They would rather earn 5% on their money than pay 15% in credit card interest. These people are the ones that you read about in the popular book a few years ago called *The Millionaire Next Door.*

They do not always drive the fanciest car, but the most practical car. Having dinner at home most of the time is fine with them. They buy clothes when needed and not for entertainment. When the stock market goes crazy for a period of time, they usually do not get too frazzled, because their portfolio is diversified and they know it goes up and down but mostly up over a long period of time. When it comes time to retire from their vocation, they still maintain an active lifestyle, because they are able to financially.

I know a couple who are now in their eighties and the husband has been retired for several years now from his job, but neither one for the Lord. She sits in front of her window every morning and every afternoon praying for the high school kids who walk by their home.

She gets excited telling of all the stories, how they scrimped and saved when they were younger and how they refused to go in

---

The people who are financially secure are the ones who would rather earn interest than pay interest.

---

debt. It is entertaining when she tells me how she still doesn't like being invested in the stock market because it can be so risky. It's funny because *she* has been the one investing in mutual funds for more than thirty years and now has investments totaling over $1 million.

This book started off as an extension of the workshops I was doing for churches. In no way can this be considered a complete volume on your finances. There are hundreds of books on personal finances but I don't know of one that incorporates God's Word in the vast world of financial planning like this one. This really is *The Lord's Financial Plan.*

This can be a valuable tool to get started. To create the correct mindset of being a good financial steward, of knowing what the Lord expects from us, of being aware of the tools available, and to have a giving attitude. My hope is that the readers would incorporate what they have learned and not just let the information become stagnant.

James 1: 22-25   *But be doers of the word, and not hearers only, deceiving yourselves. For if anyone is a hearer of the word and not a doer, he is like a man observing his natural face in a mirror; for he observes himself, goes away, and immediately forgets what kind of man he was. But he who looks into the perfect law of liberty and continues in it, and is not a forgetful hearer but a doer of the work, this one will be blessed in what he does.*

Be doers and not just hearers. That last line in verse 25 says it all. Everyone wants to be blessed, and who does not want God Almighty to be the one doing the blessing? Pastor Charles Stanley of In Touch ministries writes:

"Following God's will shifts our focus from disobedience's consequences to obedience's blessings. Once we taste the best He has to offer, we want to keep good flowing into our lives. Obedience and God's best are natural partners – good derives from following divine commands, while suffering results when we stubbornly choose our own way. This irrevocable principle plays out in the Bible as well as in day-to-day life. Every act of obedience is rewarded – either on earth or in Heaven. As we become more aware of how blessing follows obedience, we realize that complying with the Lord's will is the only wise choice."

I used to love going to seminars with subjects that were interesting to me and did not cost anything to go. I would always learn something about the topic; such as asset protection, real estate investing, or even buying options in the stock market. As we all know, nothing worthwhile is free (except of course God's forgiveness, grace, mercy, and salvation), and the seminar presenters would try to sell their programs at the end of the seminar.

People have a tendency to get real ecstatic at the end of a seminar and buy the materials off their emotion. Here is a little secret of mine. I would ask the people who bought the program for their phone number. I'd tell them I wasn't buying today and if I could call and ask their opinion about the tapes after they listened to them.

I would wait 3 or 4 months and call the people and guess what? Some of the people never even opened the package, while some others might have listened to the beginning of the tapes but they never finished. I would offer to buy them for pennies on the dollar and I would get all these great learning materials for a fraction of the cost.

My point is after reading this book, please implement what you learned. This is just to get you going. In the workshops, I try to get people to start tithing, even if it is only a quarter tithe the first time. At the end of the four weeks, I was asking people to trust God for the whole tithe. Can we trust the Lord for a month? We've given Him our soul, can we give Him our money?

I recently met a very Godly single mother who is 62 years old. She wants to retire in four years so she can receive the maximum amount from Social Security. She started late in her retirement planning and only has about $24,000 in her company's 401(k) plan. However, she has been faithfully tithing well above 10% since she rededicated her life in 1996. She holds fast to the promises of God and has complete confidence in Him.

The hotel where she works as an executive assistant to the president sold this year to a large conglomerate. The president wanted to give her a bonus for her hard work all these years. He is not a Christian and never wanted to give her a bonus previously because he told her, "I know you're just going to give it to some church." The amount of this bonus was incredibly higher than any pre-conceived sum she might have had. Incidentally, at the same time, the new president gave her a 12% pay increase to stay with the new company, and allowed her to keep her seniority and her four weeks of paid vacation every year.

She will tithe on the gross amount of this very large gift from her old boss to her church. She is going to pay off her car loan, do some home repairs, pay for her son's doctorate program while he teaches at a Christian school, and invest the rest for her future.

This future, which was pretty bleak earlier this year, will now include serving the Lord on a full time basis when she turns 66 years old. Her retirement income will be plenty for the rest of her life because she lives a simple and practical life. Her home will almost be paid in full. And, she'll still be able to pass on and give from an estate that will be worth almost seven figures. Talk about a legacy!

All the credit goes to our Heavenly Father who loves us and wants to bless us. This wonderful Christian woman just can't stop praising God for His faithfulness. She always knew that God would take care of her and her son, but never in her wildest dreams did she think He would do something this amazing.

Do a budget and find where the money is going. *Figure* out your net worth to get a starting point. *Create* a system for your family that can be easily taught to others. *Stay* out of debt by living within your means. *Learn* to be content, for Godliness with contentment is great gain. *Leave* a legacy.

You will require professional help getting the right amount of insurance with the best company for your *protection*. The same with the *accumulation* and investing, a trusted financial advisor will be needed. An estate-planning attorney is the only way to have the proper legal documents drawn up for the *preservation* section in your life.

The three major sections of financial planning: protection, accumulation, and preservation are explained spiritually and practically. My hope in writing this book is that the concept of Biblical financial stewardship will become engrained in your life and the desire to give in your hearts. You will come to realize how much you can trust our Lord and how much He wants us to trust Him.

> Psalm 28:7   *The Lord is my strength and my shield;*
> *My heart trusted in Him, and I am helped; Therefore*
> *my heart greatly rejoices, and with my song I will*
> *praise Him.*

My Testimony

Luke 7:41 - 43

"There was a certain creditor who had two debtors. One owed five hundred denari, and the other fifty. And when they had nothing with which to repay, he freely forgave them both. Tell Me, therefore, which of them will love him more?" Simon answered and said, "I suppose the one whom he forgave more." And He said to him "You have rightly judged."

The Lord has blessed my career as a Financial Planner and some would consider me a successful entrepreneur. I've owned, bought, started, and partnered dozens of companies in several different industries. I have spoken to thousands of people regarding their money through workshops and seminars. I have served and still serve on many boards and committees. I started investing at an early age and always knew I'd be around wealth and finances.

The problem with the above paragraph was the same problem I had before I became a Christian. It was a pride problem. It was all about me, my, and I. God used all these experiences, plus several trials and tribulations to get me to where I am today – a place that serves God with compassion and with a humble heart. This pilgrimage had me go to the absolute bottom before I could be of any use for Him.

The Lord impressed upon me to write this book to help people with their money and stewardship. However, this chapter was written to show everyone how God can use anyone for His glory.

I hear many testimonies as Chairman of our weekly Christian Business Fellowship meetings. Some are good and some are not so good. Ideally a testimony should be divided into three parts: 1) how you were before Christ entered your heart, 2) How you came to know Jesus as your Savior, and 3) What God has done in your life since your conversion.

Similar to Paul speaking to King Agrippa in Acts in the 26th chapter. Like Paul, I want to appeal to the non-believer. My desire would be the same response given by King Agrippa, "You almost persuade me to become a Christian."

The late baseball player Lou Gehrig once made the now famous statement, "I consider myself the luckiest man on the face of the earth." He said this shortly after learning he had a fatal disease and he was going to die soon. I also believe I am one of the luckiest men in the world.

I was born illegitimately and given up for adoption by my natural or biological mother who was Catholic and didn't believe in abortions. The same doctor who delivered me was also my adoptive parent's doctor. My "new" mom was in the hospital and going through her fourth miscarriage.

The doctor felt so bad for my parents and their loss, especially since he personally felt he should have done something medically to save this last baby, that he asked if they had ever considered adopting. The reason, he said, was that he just delivered a beautiful baby boy that was going to be put up for adoption, and if they were interested, he'd ask the mom if I could go home with them. My parents were all of a sudden very interested in adopting.

My natural mother said yes, but the only requirement was that I had to be raised Catholic. My parents, who had never been in a Catholic church prior to this and to my knowledge still haven't been in a Catholic church, said "OK." I went home two days later with my parents and I did not go through the normal adoption process. I am named after the doctor, Joseph McDaniel.

So I was born a bastard and my new parents were liars. That's how I began this wonderful holiday on earth. There were complications with the adoption later, however. After I was home with my adoptive parents for about six months, my natural mother had reconciled with her husband and was back living with him in Chicago. I was born in Los Angeles. They decided they wanted me back even though her husband was not my natural father. There was a court date set and this was to determine when I would go back to my natural mother – not if, but when.

One week before the court date, the husband had a heart attack and died. The judge said it would be better to leave things as they were. So I was able to stay with my mom and dad. Coincidentally, they had their own child two years later and my sister's name is Naomi.

Ever since I was a little boy, I wanted to be rich and famous. I loved baseball and I thought that would be the avenue for my fame and fortune. But what I really loved more than anything else was the idea of having a lot of money. I saved every penny and had the uncanny ability to find money anywhere and everywhere.

One time, our house was robbed while my parents were away and my sister and I were staying at my cousin's. The thieves broke open my piggy bank and stole all the change. I was crushed! Luckily, however, all the bills were still stuck on the sides of the piggy bank and the crooks didn't see them. My parents had a harder time telling me about my piggy bank than about the TV, stereo, jewelry, and everything else taken.

I started earning an allowance at an early age: cleaning the pool daily, taking care of our dogs, and mowing the lawns. It didn't take long to figure out I could make even more money by mowing other people's lawns also. So on Saturdays, I would push my dad's lawnmower up and down the streets finding yards that needed cut. People probably thought I was quite the enterprising kid more than they needed their lawns mowed.

Another way I made money was to paint street addresses on the curbs with a kit I had put together. If I wanted a new deck for my skateboard, for example, I would take a friend with me and paint 5 or 6 house addresses and then go buy a new "stick."

I always had cash in my pocket and friends around me. It holds true today that if you have a lot of money you have a lot of friends. I was the one who paid for the movie tickets, the beef jerky, ice cream, and admission to the skateboard parks. In the movie, Spiderman, the uncle says to Peter, "With great power comes great responsibility." I had the "power" to earn money at an early age and I give my parents all the credit for keeping me somewhat humble. I had a lot of friends, but they were very good kids and I never got into serious trouble.

In 7th grade, I was the president of the school's lapidary club. I made so many rings, necklaces, bookends, clocks, and paperweights that I didn't know what to do with them all. So I went to our neighborhood jewelry store and made a deal with the owner. He gave me a 4-foot glass display to sell all my stuff. I learned about profit margins and the concept of consignment from this kind old man.

To say I was consumed about money would be an understatement. It became a running joke in my family. One day on one of my cousin's birthday, my grandma had given him a present. When he opened it and saw it was a Bible, he was less than enthused and set it down. I picked it up and my grandma started to squirm. Sure enough, I found the $20.00 hidden in one of the pages. If there was money around, everyone knew I would find it.

Another time, a different cousin came home from the school across the street where we were playing. He set four pennies on the table and was asked where he got those. He said, "Joey was throwing them away and I picked them up."

He was sent to his room for a timeout for lying, because my aunt knew I loved money so much that I would never throw money away, even pennies. In fact, I was throwing them at a basketball hoop in the playground when he picked them up.

I did not grow up in a Christian home, but it was not dysfunctional in any way, either. We lived a wonderful, loving, hardworking lifestyle. With that in mind, my mom visited a psychic for advice on several occasions. This lady fortuneteller, Rita, told my mom that I would be an extremely successful businessman and own lots of valuable property. Since I didn't know any better, I believed this with my whole heart, up until I became a Christian at 30 years of age. I did buy some property, but it never became what I had always envisioned by this fortune-teller.

This is an example of the power of suggestion, having family and friends continually telling me about my ability to make money, my believing a fortuneteller, and earning an income at a young age. I really did believe earning money was a special gift to me and that I would naturally get better at it as I grew older.

The sky was the limit. I opened my first savings account when I was eight years old. I started looking at stock charts in the newspaper trying to figure out how to make money by investing when I was ten, right after I read about the Los Angeles Dodgers, of course. I just knew I would be very rich and famous.

Sometimes our family would go to Sunday School at a Baptist church in Glendora, California where I grew up, but not very often. But when I was thirteen years old, my parents told my sister and me we were all getting baptized at a Mormon church. We became very active Mormons for about three years. My dad started tithing for the first time and his business prospered, we had a two-year supply of food, and did all the "normal" practices of a good Mormon family.

When I started high school, things changed radically. I was very serious about baseball and was working six days a week for my dad at his gas station. I had many new friends, kids who were popular, others that partied, the jocks, and the cheerleaders. We stopped going to church, I bought my first car when I turned sixteen, and I started partying. And as my dad says, "It was all girls and gasoline" for the next ten years.

I moved out and started college when I was seventeen, a month before my eighteenth birthday. I was now working part-time for a grocery store and still working for my dad. Work, party, study, play baseball, and sleep occasionally was my lifestyle.

I moved up very quickly at the grocery store and was a third stage journeyman earning over $12.00 an hour by the time I was nineteen years old. I had now realized I was not nearly good enough to play baseball for a living and was only playing in college to get the classes and schedule I wanted. A friend I had known since kindergarten owned a convenience store and was doing great financially. I told him if he ever wanted to expand, I'd leave the grocery store and work with him. My dad thought I was crazy for even considering this.

Two years later the call from my friend came and I left the grocery store, the union, my pension, a chance to manage a store myself, and my college units to work with my friend. My dad was beside himself. He could not believe I would give up such a promising career to work at an independent store without anything close to a retirement plan.

My dad was self-employed the majority of his life and he had gone through some terrible times. He thought the best thing for me was to work for a company my whole life and retire comfortably.

However, that was never my mindset. I knew the only way to make the serious cash was working for yourself. My friend was driving a new Porsche, owned a condominium, and had all the fun toys a 21-year-old man wants. That was the lifestyle I was after.

Everything I learned from the grocery store, which was a major chain, I incorporated into this convenience store. We doubled the sales my first year. We doubled them again my second year. I wish it were all because I am a genius, but the population in the immediate area also had grown. We were able to expand and opened many other stores, and I was a partner in all the new stores.

My partner was able to get into another industry, which I originally did not care for, called check cashing. My partner was now making way too much money for a 25-year-old. We were very immature, selfish, and had absolutely no accountability at all, but I was living the life that I had always envisioned.

At the same time I invented an industry that had never been done before as far as I know. I read once that if you can make a business out of your hobby, than you would never have to go to "work" again. So I started an indoor batting cage business for baseball and softball players that took off like crazy. I was thinking that I could go out on my own and not run all these other stores anymore. Even though I was making a great income and had equity in many businesses, I was working too many hours. Typical days were opening a store at 6 a.m. and run around like a madman all day, then close my batting cages at 10 p.m. This went on for almost four years.

During this time, my girlfriend, Adria, got pregnant and had a baby girl. We named her Alexa Rae. From the instant I saw her, everything changed! Money, prestige, ego, pride, toys, business all took a back seat. I cannot explain it properly. My whole life had been centered on how much money can I make? At that moment it changed to how can I be the best dad to this precious little girl.

I thought about how much my dad sacrificed to raise me. How important it was to my mom and dad to see every baseball game, every award ceremony, and every special event in my life. I was thinking that, with my schedule, I would not see my daughter grow up. Something had to change.

I decided I have to be a responsible citizen now and stop thinking so much about me. So I proposed to Adria on New Year's Eve at midnight and we were married on April Fool's Day. Alexa was in our wedding. Nobody in their right mind thought this marriage would work.

Deep down, I probably didn't think so either. I didn't really care because I never took anything too serious anyway. I was just a carefree knucklehead. But, I sure loved my daughter. I then bought a house and had another gorgeous daughter named Jayme Rose. I remember thinking I'll never be able to love someone else as much as I already love Alexa, but as soon as I saw Jayme, my love capacity instantly doubled.

Things were changing all right. However, not all the changes were good. My batting cages that were doing so well in the beginning were going down in sales, because in every nearby town other people decided to open their own indoor batting cages. They were like post offices – one in every city. This was very flattering, but terrible to the bottom line.

Since I knew how hard this business was, and I did not need to make a profit at this business, I decided to wait for my competition to go under. At the same time, I was expanding the retail side of the batting cages by selling baseball and softball equipment. With the quantities of gear I was purchasing, I was able to be less expensive than all the major sporting goods stores. However, that took another toll on the cash flow.

The other challenge was my partner was having trouble managing his check cashing stores and asked me to take over the management of these stores. I agreed to do this if I could have free reign to run them the way I thought they should be run, and if I could be 50/50 partners in the equity. He thought this was fair and it gave him the time he wanted to devote to his newest venture, a self-serve carwash.

So now I am working even harder and longer and not making any more money. What I was gaining in equity in one side was not making up for the loss in the other. All the time I was thinking I was doing this to actually free up time to spend with my new little family.

I cannot remember how many employees I had at this time, but one was my sister, Naomi. She worked almost every day with a part-time employee who was also a pastor, at one of the check cashing centers. Eventually, Naomi became a Christian. And not one of the run-of-the-mill Christians, either. She was a sold-out, "born-again," on-fire, pray-every-chance-you-get "Jesus freak." I thought she was in a cult. I wanted nothing to do with her after that. But

Naomi started praying for me along with all the other Christians that worked for me, and I didn't even know about it.

I finally relented to go to church with them after a year of them bugging me. It was a small Pentecostal church that these employees all went to. I thought Naomi was part of a cult before, but I *knew* she was after attending the service. There were people standing up, clapping in church, and there was even a band. People were talking in strange languages. One man started prophesying of things to come. None of this happened at our Mormon church. Only out of sheer embarrassment did I not leave in the middle of the service. When the pastor started his sermon I thought, finally someone normal.

The pastor's message was on the responsibilities of a husband in the letter to the Ephesians. I didn't even know there was an Ephesians in the Bible. I thought it was Mathew, Mark, Luke, John, and Revelations. I was so convicted that I thought Naomi called the pastor and said my brother is coming Sunday, can you do a talk on husbands and marriage.

I remember thinking, "Why would he alienate all these people on account of me?" I was so full of myself, so much pride, and so arrogant. I really did believe my mom, who said I was a very special boy!

I had always read self-help books, went to motivational seminars, and listened to hundreds of tapes in my car about being the best I can be. I am sure I was closer to being a "New Age" believer in a higher power than believing in a personal God. But the pastor's message really hit me and I wanted to hear more.

The only problem was I would have to come back the next week. After four consecutive Sundays, I went up to the front and accepted Jesus as my Savior and Lord. All my sins past, present, and future are now erased, "just as if I have never sinned" is what the pastor said. Complete forgiveness by God, because of what Jesus did on the cross is the only way to Heaven and eternal life. I was thirty years old.

Prior to this, I would have thought I'd go to Heaven because I was a decent person. I mean except for my smut mouth, the alcohol, and my deviant behavior, I'm a good guy – or so I thought. I never hurt anyone, I didn't steal, and I always paid my taxes.

Then I thought back to the time I got a girl pregnant when I was nineteen and she had an abortion. I didn't even think of another option. I was more upset about paying the $275 than I was about killing a baby. The mother's physical and emotional pain was not considered or contemplated very much, either. If anyone should have had sympathy to save a baby from death by abortion it should have been me. My maternal mother could have had an abortion with me and I wouldn't be here today. How could I have let this tragedy happen! I never *hurt* anyone? How many thousands of times have I hurt someone?

I think about the times I took advantage of a little kid who was taking his dad's collectable coins and bringing them to me at the store and I would give the kid a large soda and a candy bar. I stole his father's gift to his son someday. I don't steal? How many times have I stolen something, tangible and intangible, to satisfy my own selfish desires? I do not even want to mention a word about taxes on the grounds that I might incriminate myself.

One sin and I would not be allowed in Heaven and I had literally hundreds of thousands of them, and now they all were forgiven because of Jesus. Sometimes it is too much to comprehend. Our God is so merciful that I cannot help but praise Him and serve Him.

My challenge now was how I was going to explain this to my wife. She thought Naomi was weirder than I did, and now I am one of them.

I started taking my two daughters to church every Sunday but Adria refused to go. She was probably thinking about all the stuff we were going to give up if we all became Christians.

At that time in our lives we had Dodger, Laker, and Kings season tickets, including all the concerts at the Fabulous Forum, and the after parties in the Forum Club with the celebrities. It was a fun time to be a fan in the eighties and nineties in Los Angeles. We had Lasorda, Magic, Kareem, Gretzgy, and world championships almost every year. It was a decade long party and it seemed like we were the hosts.

It was the toughest year I had ever experienced in my marriage and my life up to this point. About that time my pastor started a "Friday Fast" for the church and so I decided to try fasting for the first time.

My life that seemed so invincible earlier now seemed to be out of control. My parents were divorcing after 31 years of marriage. My partner had already divorced and was partying way too much and was never at work. The check-cashing centers' sales were dropping dramatically because the major banks entered the industry for the first time. My batting cages had not been profitable for a few years now, I was wearing out physically, and my marriage was on the rocks. When Adria found out I was fasting, she went berserk. She said, "I knew you would become a Jesus freak!"

Ironically, that Friday set a record for my largest one-day sales volume at the batting cages. Adria and I didn't talk that Friday and I stayed at work till after 11:00 that night. Saturday morning as she was leaving to open one of the stores, we kissed and made up.

The next day, Sunday, she was getting dressed up and I asked her where she was going. She answered, "I want to go with you guys to church." I started to cry right then and there. Every time I tell this story I get choked up. Even as I write this now it affects me. God is such a loving God! I have been a believer in fasting ever since. I have seen God do amazing things through the power of prayer and fasting. I still fast on most Fridays.

It took a little longer for Adria to ask Jesus into her heart, but she did after about four months. Now we were a family going to church every Sunday, together at last. I still had my business troubles though, and they had to be dealt with.

I decided I couldn't manage all that was going on and be home with my family, so I started to sell the businesses. I started to feel dirty selling beer, alcohol, lottery tickets, and cigarettes after awhile, even though the stores were very classy and clean. They had delicatessens in them and always had great prices. We were the corner market and served the community very well. I felt as though God wanted me to do something else, however.

It took about three years to sell off the markets only keeping the one that my partner originally had before I came along. I had a real problem with selling the batting cages, though. It was such a specialized business and not just anybody could run it, plus the fact it wasn't showing a profit didn't help matters, either. And without the income from the other businesses, I was starting to lose a lot of money.

This was very difficult to accept. I wasn't the hotshot I thought I was. It seemed as though everything business-wise was crumbling. I had read all the business books, listened to all the motivational tapes, I set goals – I was doing everything right on the outside. And to everyone else who saw, it looked as though I was doing great. It was the biggest facade.

I didn't plan it this way; it was just people's perception of me. Young guy, beautiful wife, happy children, lots of businesses – he's got it made. But all this incredible pressure I put on myself got to the point where I considered suicide. I was so hard on myself that I could not stand the thought of failing, of letting my wife down, of disappointing so many people. I look back now and it sounds so ridiculous to be so worried about other people's view of me.

Eventually, I found a buyer for the batting cages, which was a miracle in itself; the story is too long to tell, however, God really saved me from financial disaster. I ended up selling it for what I put into it to start the venture. The corporation that bought the batting cages got the deal of a lifetime.

When I first opened the batting cages, I had many offers from potential buyers and I would listen to the offers and then say no. It was a pride issue for me. I was only 25 years old when I started it, and I thought I was such a big-time businessman.

There were many major leaguers who would come in during their off season and use it. I held many special events there and I would get my picture in the newspaper. It was a good feeling when mayors of cities would ask a favor from me – to reserve a spot for them during the peak season. It was all a big ego trip for me in the beginning and so much a humbling experience in the end.

After all this time had passed, I was manager of a convenience store and part owner of a three-store chain of check cashing centers that were declining in value more and more. My partner was now in the carwash business full-time and making a real good income. He was still partying heavily and I wanted nothing to do with it. I told him I wanted to dissolve the partnership so I could do other things, thinking he could get his life back together by working at his business again. I told him that I would stay for three months to get the operation ready for him to take over.

He did not take this news very well at all, and we had a very ugly breakup. What I thought was admirable, he took as betrayal. So two weeks after I was his best man at his second wedding and two days after my now fourth child and second son, Noah, was born, I did not have a job, income, or equity. My only consolation was that at least now, Lucas, my first son, had a younger brother.

My partner, my friend of 31 years, never paid me my share of the businesses that he had promised to me. The reasons I stuck around, through all his nonsense and personal problems, was that I thought I was his only real and true friend, and to have something monetarily at the end of our partnership. Now I had nothing.

Now at the time, I was thinking, "It's only money." Well, it's only money until you don't have any, then it becomes pretty important. Money is not the most important thing, but it's right up there with air.

I thought I'd take a month off to try to relax and regroup, thinking this was my time to try the corporate world and find out if I am as good as I think I am. I did not have a degree. I did not have legitimate computer skills. I was a self-employed maverick who made too much income in the eyes of the corporate people. I could not get a job.

There is nothing as discouraging to a man as realizing that he cannot support his family. I had been through some rough times in the past few years, but nothing compared to not being able to find work. I got very depressed at times and started to complain about my life.

We lived off our savings and investments for a year and for the first time in my life, I had no money. Since I could not find a job, I decided that God must want me to open another company. So I started a food distribution company that sold chicken to Kentucky Fried Chicken restaurants, and for the first time, with borrowed money.

This venture took six months to set up. In the ensuing six months, the business did better than expected. After the first month, it was a million-dollar business. I thought God was blessing me for all my hard work, sacrifice, and devotion to Him. I knew He would never leave me, but in my mind, He was rewarding me for not leaving *Him* after all these trials and tribulations. One month later, my chicken supplier negotiated with KFC and phased me out, and my business was over.

What was happening to me? Nothing was working. I was the Boy Wonder once. Everything I touched turned a profit. I used to say that all that business needs is a little bit of Joe. Now I couldn't make anything work. If I threw a quarter in the air, it came down a nickel. God, what are you doing to me? I tithe, I give, and I am trying to be the best steward I can be. What do you want me to do? I'll do anything you want me to, just tell me!

This time I had no income, no job, no equity, no savings, and had an enormous amount of debt. I did finally find a job in food sales, after six more months of trying to keep my business open by selling food to anyone, mainly grocery stores. By this time, however, I had lost almost everything.

The Lord tells us in Proverbs 16:18

Pride goes before destruction, and a haughty spirit before a fall.

I had a lot of pride, so there was a lot of destruction. I also had a gigantic haughty spirit, so there was a gigantic fall. I was modest when people praised me for my accomplishments, but deep down I really thought I was incredibly gifted.

I was even proud about my ability to be a family man. What more can I do to please my beautiful wife and children? I listen to my wife, I am romantic, and we go places together. I read to my kids, coach their teams, and give nice gifts. I don't go out with the boys, drink, smoke, or gamble, and I'm home every night for dinner. What more could any woman want?

Well, for one thing, they want security. They want to know there will be a home to sleep in. They want to have food in the pantry for the children. They do not want to be a charity case to their friends and family. They want the security of knowing the husband will be OK emotionally and is the strong anchor he is supposed to be.

My wife could not handle all the change of events in such a short period of time, and left the kids and me. There was our personal financial ruin, there were several family members who died, and there was divorce, cancer, sickness, and disorders. In my mind, these are the events that make you stronger; these are the chapters in life that will make a great book someday. But it was too much for her. I could not do my food sales job any more because I was away from the house too much and could not take care of my children. My youngest son had just turned three years old.

So a friend suggested I go into financial planning. Unlimited income, make my own schedule and you get to help people – it sounded so promising. I didn't know much about the industry. Years earlier I studied to become a counselor for Christian

Financial Concepts, now called Crown Ministries. I thought I'd become this wealthy businessman and be able to help Christians in all their finances. Just come and sit at my feet and learn from the all-knowing wise business guru. But after studying for the courses, I realized it was not enough information to be the counselor I envisioned and I did not pursue it any further.

After I talked to different financial companies and understood their training program and how I'd be able to help people, I could not wait to get started. What I didn't realize was how hard the industry tests were to get my stockbroker and registered investment advisor licenses.

I praise God for getting me through them and all the while going through my intense heartache. I was completely broke financially, my heart was shattered, and my poor children having to go through this mess, too. They had nothing to do with this disaster and they are the ones who have to live through it and somehow learn to make sense of it. Without the prayers of my church body and my close Christian friends, I know I would not be here today.

It was an extremely difficult time in my life and there were times when I didn't think I was going to make it. I didn't want to make it, I really wanted to just lay down and die. I know now what living day-to-day means. I used to think it was a silly cliché. It became hour-to-hour and then I was calling on Jesus every minute to help me get to the next minute. You cannot help but get close to God when you are crying out to Him every second.

The Lord has made me a new creation. There were some wild and crazy ways for several years. I had fast cars, boats, motorcycles, four-wheel drives, sports gear, and all the extra toys available. My friends and I really thought we were the "Man's Man" and we played it to the hilt. There was always a party at my house. We made, spent, and wasted a lot of money on wine, women, and song, but God protected me all those years. Through all the car crashes, motorcycle accidents, and all the stupid stunts I pulled to be a showoff, the Lord was there watching over me. He saved me and has a wonderful plan for my life. And now He has given me the awesome responsibility of raising two daughters and two sons.

James Allen, in his book As a Man Thinketh, says, "The purpose of suffering is to purify, to burn out all that is useless and impure. There is no reason to continue burning gold after the dross has been removed." There was suffering and God knows exactly what He is doing with every single person He has created, and He would not give me any more than I could handle.

Now I feel like David did when he wrote Psalm 30:11, 12:

> *You have turned my mourning into dancing; You have put off my sackcloth and clothed me with gladness, to the end that my soul may sing praise to You and not be silent. O Lord my God, I will give thanks to You forever.*

My testimony is God's testimony of His perfect love and faithfulness. It is an example of how God uses all people and all circumstances to bring Him glory. I am now a financial planner for the Christian Community Credit Union, and it is the joy of my life. I'm able to do things I never thought possible. I used to think that I was going to be a motivational speaker. Now I am speaking on topics that will last a lifetime – not the temporary rush of trying to motivate someone.

I thought I had to own businesses to be a businessman. But now I understand dozens of industries and I have much more business acumen and understanding now than I ever would in trying to be the owner of a company. I am able to help families, churches, and ministries understand God's Word regarding their financial stewardship.

Now I realize how God is able to use me. I would never have chosen this route to get where I am today, nor would I want anybody to go through it themselves. However, it was God's perfect plan for *my* life. I needed to learn some valuable life lessons that I wouldn't have learned any other way. I used to think I wanted to be rich and famous. And I am rich today. I don't mean monetarily, but rich where it counts, and that is in Heaven. And as long as I am famous in my children's eyes, that is enough fame for me.

> John 14:2, 3 *"In my Father's house are many mansions; if it were not so, I would have told you. I go to prepare a place for you. And if I go and prepare a place for you, I will come again and receive you to Myself; that where I am, there you may be also."*

About the Author

Joseph E. Singleton entered the financial planning industry in 2000 after almost seventeen years of entrepreneurship, where he bought, sold, and started dozens of businesses. He and his team currently help hundreds of families, churches, and ministries with their money management. Joseph is also the Director of Storehouse Ministries at Pomona First Baptist Church – a ministry that educates, facilitates, and motivates financial stewardship. He brings awareness of Biblical financial planning through workshops and seminars to other churches and ministries as well.

However, the road to this point in Joseph's life has not been a gentle ride. He lost everything once and on the way up again, lost it all a second time. The second devastation was even more painful than the first. He understands the despair of immense debt and the lost feeling of extreme loneliness. But God has a plan that is the very best, which will always happen when you are completely surrendered to Him.

Joseph lives with his four children, Alexa, Jayme, Lucas, and Noah, in Southern California.

Joseph can be reached at the Christian Community
Credit Union at (800) 930-3642